Battleground E[...]

CW00960370

DAS RE[...]

2nd SS Panzer Division *Das Reich* – Drive to Normandy, June 1944

Other guides in the Battleground Europe Series:

Walking the Salient *by* Paul Reed
Ypres - Sanctuary Wood and Hooge *by* Nigel Cave
Ypres - Hill 60 *by* Nigel Cave
Ypres - Messines Ridge *by* Peter Oldham
Ypres - Polygon Wood *by* Nigel Cave
Ypres - Passchendaele *by* Nigel Cave
Ypres - Airfields and Airmen *by* Michael O'Connor

Walking the Somme *by* Paul Reed
Somme - Gommecourt *by* Nigel Cave
Somme - Serre *by* Jack Horsfall & Nigel Cave
Somme - Beaumont Hamel *by* Nigel Cave
Somme - Thiepval *by* Michael Stedman
Somme - La Boisselle *by* Michael Stedman
Somme - Fricourt *by* Michael Stedman
Somme - Carnoy-Montauban *by* Graham Maddocks
Somme - Pozieres *by* Graham Keech
Somme - Courcelette *by* Paul Reed
Somme - Boom Ravine *by* Trevor Pidgeon
Somme - Mametz Wood *by* Michael Renshaw
Somme - Delville Wood *by* Nigel Cave
Somme - Advance to Victory (North) 1918 *by* Michael Stedman

Arras - Vimy Ridge *by* Nigel Cave
Arras - Gavrelle *by* Trevor Tasker and Kyle Tallett
Arras - Bullecourt *by* Graham Keech
Arras - Monchy le Preux *by* Colin Fox

Hindenburg Line *by* Peter Oldham
Hindenburg Line Epehy *by* Bill Mitchinson
Hindenburg Line Riqueval *by* Bill Mitchinson
Hindenburg Line Villers-Plouich *by* Bill Mitchinson
Hindenburg Line - Cambrai *by* Jack Horsfall & Nigel Cave
Hindenburg Line - Saint Quentin *by* Helen McPhail and Philip Guest

La Bassée - Neuve Chapelle *by* Geoffrey Bridger

Mons *by* Jack Horsfall and Nigel Cave

Accrington Pals Trail *by* William Turner

Poets at War: Wilfred Owen *by* Helen McPhail and Philip Gues
Poets at War: Edmund Blunden *by* Helen McPhail and Philip Gu

Gallipoli *by* Nigel Steel

Italy - Asiago *by* Francis Mackay

Boer War - The Relief of Ladysmith *by* Lewis Childs
Boer War - The Siege of Ladysmith *by* Lewis Childs
Boer War - Kimberley *by* Lewis Childs
Isandlwana *by* Ian Knight and Ian Castle
Rorke's Drift *by* Ian Knight and Ian Castle

WW2 **Pegasus Bridge/Merville Battery** *by* Carl Shilleto
WW2 **Gold Beach** *by* Christopher Dunphie & Garry Johnson
WW2 **Omaha Beach** *by* Tim Kilvert-Jones
WW2 **Battle of the Bulge - St Vith** *by* Michael Tolhurst
WW2 **Dunkirk** *by* Patrick Wilson
WW2 **Calais** *by* John Cooksey
WW2 **Das Reich – Drive to Normandy** *by* Philip Vickers
WW2 **Hill 112** *by* Tim Saunders

Battleground Europe Series guides under contract for future release:
Somme - High Wood *by* Terry Carter
Somme - Ginchy *by* Michael Stedman
Somme - Combles *by* Paul Reed
Somme - Beaucourt *by* Michael Renshaw
Walking Arras *by* Paul Reed
Hougoumont *by* Julian Paget and Derek Saunders

With the continued expansion of the Battleground series a
Battleground Series Club has been formed to benefit the reader. The
purpose of the Club is to keep members informed of new titles and to
offer many other reader-benefits. Membership is free and by
registering an interest you can help us predict print runs and thus assist
us in maintaining the quality and prices at their present levels.

Please call the office 01226 734555, or send your name and address
along with a request for more information to:
Battleground Series Club Pen & Sword Books Ltd,
47 Church Street, Barnsley, South Yorkshire S70 2AS

Battleground Europe

DAS REICH
2nd SS Panzer Division *Das Reich* – Drive to
Normandy, June 1944

Philip Vickers

LEO COOPER

COMBINED PUBLISHING
Pennsylvania

To
Vera Atkins
with my appreciation

Published by
LEO COOPER
an imprint of
Pen & Sword Books Limited
47 Church Street, Barnsley, South Yorkshire S70 2AS
Copyright © Philip Vickers 2000

ISBN 0 85052 699 X

A CIP record of this book is available
from the British Library

Printed by Redwood Books Limited
Trowbridge, Wiltshire

*For up-to-date information on other titles produced under the Leo Cooper
imprint, please telephone or write to:*
Pen & Sword Books Ltd, FREEPOST SF5, 47 Church Street
Barnsley, South Yorkshire S70 2BR
Telephone 01226 734222

Published under license in the United States of America by

COMBINED PUBLISHING

ISBN 1-58097-047-8

For information, address:
COMBINED PUBLISHING
P.O. Box 307
Conshohocken, PA 19428
E-Mail: combined@dca.net
Web: www.combinedpublishing.com
Orders: 1-800-418-6065

*Cataloging in Publication Data available from the Library of
Congress*

CONTENTS

FOREWORD
by

JACQUES R E POIRIER
DSO, Legion of Honour (Officer)
(NESTOR, CAPTAIN JACK, Chief of Circuit DIGGER)

On the morning of 8 June 1944, an immense column of tanks and armoured cars set off from a point near Montauban and headed towards us on its way to the Normandy front.

Several books have been written about the actions of the men of the *Das Reich* Division in the course of their journey northwards through the heart of France. Some writers have belittled the Resistance operations against *Das Reich*. They have failed to grasp the environment and circumstances in which men of the Maquis had to wage their unequal struggle against an elite armoured division. Our objective was to delay *Das Reich* for as long as possible by means of hit-and-run tactics and acts of sabotage. The Maquis were irregulars, not an army in the field, consequently no one should have expected them, brave and resolute though they were, to destroy or substantially diminish the fire power of one of Hitler's most experienced divisions. The Resistance did attain its objective, for it put up an admirable fight and succeeded in delaying the division by several days.

This is not a figment of my imagination. When the war ended I was informed by the British Minister of Economic Warfare, a member of Churchill's War Cabinet, that General Eisenhower had estimated that *Das Reich* had been delayed in their march north by as much as a week, due to the attacks of the Resistance.

That SS Division underwent countless attacks by our Maquis units which operated, for the most part, in small detachments: for example, JEAN PIERRE (Peter Lake), with three comrades, blew up the tracks ahead of an armoured train carrying elements of *Das Reich*. The Germans repaired the track and proceeded on their journey only to find that JEAN PIERRE had destroyed another section of track further along their route.

Most Maquis units responded to our control and mobilized to help delay the Division's drive to Normandy. The Germans themselves contributed to the delaying tactics by pursuing the maquisards into the open countryside and villages along the route instead of pressing on. No one will ever forget the massacre of the population of Oradour-sur-Glane, which was totally unjustified as no Maquis operated from there. The undeniable fact remains, *Das Reich* arrived to face the Allied troops in Normandy many days later than they would have done otehwise.

The northward march of *Das Reich* subjected the maquisards to an enormous strain, but they acquitted themselves with courage and determination. They can justly pride themselves as having made a substantial contribution to the Allied cause at a decisive stage in the war.

I would like to mention the organisation that I was proud to be a member of, the SOE (Special Operations Executive). This remarkable organi-zation united the flower of British and French youth in a common cause – the liberating of my native land. I have never felt that my service in the SOE was a form of disloyalty to General de Gaulle, for whom I had the greatest respect. On the contrary, I remain convinced that I served my country, the Allies, and the cause of freedom, far better in that efficient organisation than I would have done in any other, albeit equally courageous.

Philip Vickers has made a most laudable effort in writing such a book. I hope that British vistors to our beloved region of France will find this guide informative and interesting.

Philip, *bon vent!*

JACQUES POIRIER

ACKNOWLEDGEMENTS

I wish to express my grateful thanks to everyone who has enabled me to produce this Guide to the march of *Das Reich*.

First and foremost I wish to thank Vera Atkins for her unfailing help and advice without which this Guide would never have seen the light of day. Her award of the CBE, which came mid-way through the writing of this book, added to her *Légion D'Honneur*, was a happy and long-merited event.

Then, my sincere thanks to those SOE agents I have been honoured to meet or contact: Ralph Beauclerc, Tony Brooks, Francis Cammaerts, Gaston Collins, Pearl Cornioley, George Hiller's widow Judith Hiller, Roger Landes, Peter Lake, Peter Lee, Jacques Poirier, Brian Stonehouse, John Fielding (SAS), Hugh Verity (RAF) and Daphne Friele of the Jedburghs.

Amongst the many French Resistants who have helped I would mention: Raymond Aubrac, Jean-Bernard Badaire, Jacques de la Bardonnie, Laurette Besson, Denis Chansigaud, Louis Chaumette, La Marquise Eliane de Bermondet de Cromières, Marcelle Delord, Mme Delors, Henri & Françoise Diacano, Pierre Guthman, Georges Lachezé, Maurice Lasroux, M & Mme Robert Lecreux, Louis Saraudy, Mme Tallet, René de la Touche, Philippe Tenant de la Tour, Jacques Valéry, Marcel Verhlac and Philippe de Vomécourt's son, Alain. Also, the British Resistant, Antonia Hunt. A few have asked to remain anonymous.

My grateful thanks go also to: Donald Bittner, La Comtesse Angela Maze Sencier de Brouville, Sylvie Boudet, Pierre Combes, Richard Davies, Jacques Demoures, Paul Dixon, Lady Erroll, Harald & Sheila Folke, Arthur Layton Funk, Lucy Golder, Ian and Isabel Greig, Park Honan, Bruce Heinmark, Bruno Lédee, Yves and Agnès Lemairge Dubreuil, S J Lewis, Brigitte Manaud, Leo Marks,Paul McCue, Françoise Modéran, Richard Mullen, Severine Nicol, Jean-Christophe Olive, Jean Pelletier-Doisy, Rosemary Rigby, Kevin Ruffner, Christine Sabine, Tania Szabo, Mark Seaman, Yves Soulignac, Duncan Stuart, Nigel West and Anneliese Weidinger.

My special thanks to my wife Katharine and to my publisher.

None of the above can be held in any way responsible for any errors or omissions in this work and the author would appreciate any comments on those heads from his readers.

PHILIP VICKERS
France

INTRODUCTION

This *Battleground Europe* Guide follows the infamous Route 'B' march of the 2nd *Waffen SS* Panzer Division *Das Reich* from its headquarters in Montauban, in Tarn-et-Garonne, as far as Poitiers, in Vienne, and the SAS Operation Bulbasket, during the period 6 June to 10 July 1944.

It enables the visitor to 'see' and 'feel' for himself, even today, many of the heroic deeds of the French Resistance along the way; some of the tragedies which unfolded; and to appreciate the secret role of the British and American clandestine agents who armed, organised and in many cases led the Maquis in action.

Much of this area was called 'Little Russia' by the Germans on account of the strength of the Resistance and it was an area where the Germans and the collaborationists of Vichy were most hostile to the local population. Oradour and Tulle, towns where atrocities took place, are along the line of march.

The route lies in some of France's loveliest regions, through Quercy, the Périgord and Limousin, and touches such famous towns as Cahors, Sarlat and Limoges. It should be realised that *Das Reich* marched through this region on other routes as well, its Route 'A' being through Figeac, and a spur route to Périgueux, but Route 'B' is the principal route.

Our purpose is manifold: to bring recent history to life; to lead to an appreciation of how Britain and France worked and fought together against the common enemy; to ensure that living memory is guarded for the future (even the youngest participants of those days are now into their seventies and we are amongst the last to be able to capture their direct experiences); and to pay a tribute to both the living and the dead.

User Guide

All French map references are for the *AA Road Atlas France 2000*, 2nd Edition, January 2000 and are listed in the index. Some in-town sites have been referenced to the standard 'red' Michelin Guide, indicated 'RM'. For England the map references are for the *AA Road Atlas Great Britain 2000*, 1st Edition July 2000. In one or two instances the visitor may like to acquire the IGN '*Série Bleue*' (1cm – 250m) maps, 1930-E for

Oradour and 2130-O and 2131-E for the area around Limoges, but these are not essential, the directions in the Guide are perfectly adequate. Maps in the text are schematic. Some of the sites are on private property which must, of course, always be respected. Resistance Museums are essential orientation points. I have included a few personally selected hotels and restaurants which are particularly relevant and were, in some cases, used by SOE agents during the war.

Most importantly the visitor should always remember that many of the survivors today still bear deep personal wounds (parents shot in cold blood, homes ransacked, confidences betrayed – the march of *Das Reich* was a truly terrifying event) and not everyone is prepared to speak openly. That said, I can confirm that in the course of innumerable 'surprise visits' I have never been given anything other than the most polite and generous welcome. More than once an initially diffident start invariably developed into a genuine exchange of experiences. Without exception, being 'British' carries a real bonus, thanks to the courage and responsibility of the SOE agents whose story is, in part, told here.

Baron Philippe de Gunzbourg (EDGAR) with Maurice Loupias (BERGERET). EDGAR was WHEELWRIGHT's courier in Dordogne, later chief of Dordogne sub-region.

MAPS, CHARTS & DIAGRAMS

ABBREVIATIONS

AS	Armée Secrète
BCAR	Bureau Centrale de Reseignements et d'Action
BEF	British Expeditionary Force
CIA	Central Intelligence Agency
CDLR	Ceux de la Résistance
CN-D	Confrérie de Notre-Dame
CNR	Conseil Nationale de la Résistance
DB	Armoured Division
DI	Infantry Division
FANY	Field Ambulance Nursing Yeomanry
FFI	Forces Françaises de l'Intérieur
FTP	Francs-tireurs et Partisans
FTPF	Francs-tireurs et Partisans Français
F Section	SOE Independent French Section
Gestapo	Geheime Staatspolizei
GMR	Groupes Mobile de Réserve
M de l'H	Musée de l'Homme
MLF	Mouvement Liberté de Frenay
MLN	Mouvements de Libération Nationale
MUR	Mouvements Unis de la Résistance
MGB	Motor Gun Boat
MTB	Motor Torpedo Boat
Nazi	National Socialist Workers Party
OCM	Organisation Civile et Militaire
OG	Operational Group
ORA	Organisation de Résistance de l'Armée
OSS	Office of Strategic Services
RF Section	SOE Gaullist Section
SAS	Special Air Service
SDS	Special Duty Squadron
SHAEF	Supreme Headquarters Allied Expeditionary Force
SNCF	Société Nationale des Chemins-de-Fer Français
SOE	Special Operations Executive
SS	Schutzstaffel (Protection Squad)
STO	Service du Travail Obligatoire
WAAF	Women's Auxiliary Air Force

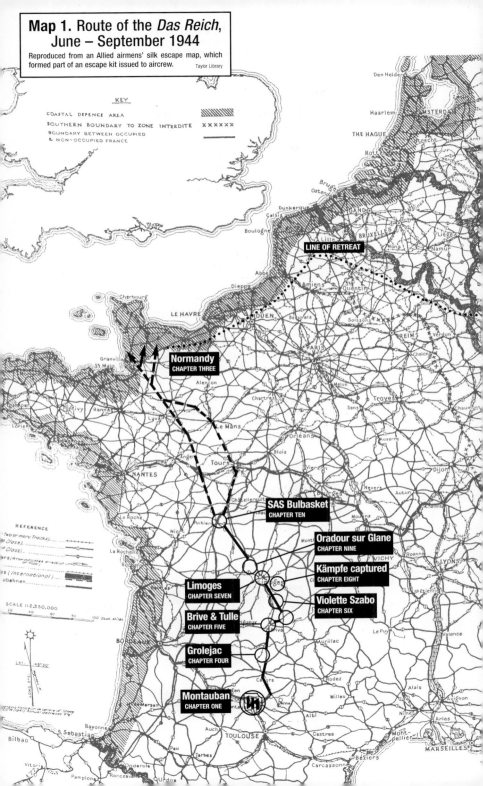

Map 1. Route of the *Das Reich*, June – September 1944

Reproduced from an Allied airmens' silk escape map, which formed part of an escape kit issued to aircrew.

Taylor Library

KEY

COASTAL DEFENCE AREA

SOUTHERN BOUNDARY TO ZONE INTERDITE xxxxx

BOUNDARY BETWEEN OCCUPIED & NON-OCCUPIED FRANCE

LINE OF RETREAT

Normandy
CHAPTER THREE

SAS Bulbasket
CHAPTER TEN

Oradour sur Glane
CHAPTER NINE

Kämpfe captured
CHAPTER EIGHT

Limoges
CHAPTER SEVEN

Violette Szabo
CHAPTER SIX

Brive & Tulle
CHAPTER FIVE

Grolejac
CHAPTER FOUR

Montauban
CHAPTER ONE

REFERENCE

SCALE 1:2,330,000

2nd SS Panzer Division Das Reich

Headquarters
Divisional Staff
Defence Company
Provost Company
8 motorcycles, 32 vehicles, 141 men

SS Panzer Regiment 2

1st Battalion
1st Panzer Company
2nd Panzer Company
3rd Panzer Company
4th Panzer Company

2nd Battalion
5th Panzer Company
6th Panzer Company
7th Panzer Company
8th Panzer Company

62 PzKw MkV Panthers, 64 PzKw MkIVs
8 Flak guns 3.7cm, 6 Flak guns 20mm
53 motorcycles
313 vehicles
2,401 men

SS Regiment 3 *Deutschland*

2nd Battalion
1st Inf Company
2nd Inf Company
3rd Inf Company
Rec Company

4th Battalion
4th Inf Company
5th Inf Company
6th Inf Company
Rec Company

88 motorcyles
527 vehicles
3,242 men

SS Regiment 4 *Der Führer*

1st Battalion
1st Inf Company
2nd Inf Company
3rd Inf Company
Rec Company

3rd Battalion
4th Inf Company
5th Inf Company
6th Inf Company
Rec Company

88 motorcyles
527 vehicles
3,242 men

SS Artillery Regiment 2

1st Battalion
1st Battery
2nd Battery
3rdBattery

2nd Battalion
4th Battery
5th Battery
6th Battery

3rd Battalion
7th Battery
8th Battery
9th Battery

4th Battalion
10th Battery
11th Battery
12th Battery

12 Howiters 17cm
6 Self-propelled guns 15cm
12 Howiters 15cm
12 Self-propelled guns 105mm
12 Howiters 105mm
40 motorcycles
534 vehicles
2,167 men

SS Flak Abteilung 2
Heavy Flak Company 88mm
Heavy Flak Company 88mm
Light Flak Company 20mm
Light Flak Company 20mm
Light Flak Company 20mm

16 motorcycles
181 vehicles
824 men

SS Pz Hunter Abteilung 2
1st Company SPG
2nd Company SPG
3rd Company

31 Self-propelled guns 75mm
12 Pak towed 40s
17 motorcycles
135 vehicles
513 men

SS StuG Abteilung 2
1st Company SPG
2nd Company SPG
3rd Company

11 motorcycles
100vehicles
344 men

SS Recon Abteilung 2
12 Self-propelled guns 75mm
35 Pak towed 20mm
6 Flamethrowers
22 motorcycles
193 vehicles
942 men

SS Nebelwrfr Abteilung 2
18 Nebelwerfers
8 motorcycles
107vehicles
473 men

SS Signals Abteilung 2
14 motorcycles
114 vehicles
515 men

SS Pioneer Abteilung 2
3 Pak towed 20/28mm
3 Pak towed 20mm
6 Flamethrowers
52 motorcycles
212 vehicles
984 men

CHAPTER ONE

2nd SS PANZER DIVISION *DAS REICH*

The Arrival of Das Reich

On 27 April 1944, the stirring strains of *Ich habe Einen Kamerade* and the rather less popular, *Horst Wessel Lied*, played by the band of the Waffen SS Panzer Grenadier Regiment *Deutschland*, crashed out in greeting of the 2nd SS Panzer Division *Das Reich* at the railway station in Toulouse.

This welcome came sweetly to the ears of the 2,500 survivors of Battle Group Lammerding, *Das Reich*, which was at the peak of Nazi Germany's best trained and most elite forces originally destined to be the spearhead of the invasion of England. Recently plucked from the ice, mud and blood of the Eastern Front, it had left behind thousands of dead in the frozen wastes of the Dnieper River basin, at Kiev and Kharkov, in the Pripet Marshes and the Cherkass pocket of Byelo-Russia and the Ukraine. Theirs was a horrendous history. In Russia and elsewhere they had cooperated with the *Einsatzgruppen* in massacres on an enormous scale: 20,000 civilians in just one 'incident' at Kharkov alone. Their journey from Russia to south west France had taken eleven days.

Hitler himself had selected Montauban, some twenty five miles to the north of Toulouse, as the designated HQ of *Das Reich* in the West. On 6 April he had pinpointed its position on a map, 'it should move over here', and his staff had confirmed its total strength at 15,385 men out of an establishment of over 20,000. Although badly mauled by the Red Army, its gaps filled by young Alsatians, Hungarians, Romanians and nine other nationalities, it was still an immensely powerful fighting force led by battle hardened veterans, brutalised by the wholesale butchery and excessive reprisals of the war without rules waged in Russia.

The sullen crowd of French people watching their march to barracks and, later, their move to the Montauban area, included the majority, the stoically indifferent; amongst the minorities, those quickly seduced by the banners, drums, decorations and

15

Men of *Das Reich* arrive in southern France from the Eastern Front.

uniforms of a seemingly glamorous and undoubtedly courageous body of fighting men; and those who, in the war in the shadows, were to be responsible for *Das Reich*'s sometimes uncomfortable stay in south west France and its subsequent nightmare march to Normandy following D-Day. It is this march we are about to follow.

Setting the Ground Plan

From the Allied viewpoint, the French Resistance organisations and the British agents of Special Operations Executive (SOE), who had been parachuted in previously, were up against a formidable German presence in the area. This force was augmented by Russian Cossack units, Lithuanians and elements of Italian Marines. As well as *Das Reich*, a regular *Wehrmacht* Armoured Division was located south of Périgueux and six Infantry Divisions were scattered across the area between Bordeaux and Cahors, all under the

General von Blaskowitz commander of Army Group G.

command of General von Blaskowitz, Army Group G, headquartered at Toulouse. This gave the Germans an approximate strength of at least 112,500 men with an unimaginable weight of armour and firepower. As the British agent NESTOR, Jacques Poirier of Circuit DIGGER, was to tell me: 'There were Germans everywhere'.

The SS Background

But to form an impression of *Das Reich*, which was part of the SS, one needs to have a brief summary of the history of the SS itself.

The SS (*Schutzstaffel*) was essentially the private domain of *Reichführer* Heinrich Himmler and was considered as his 'private property' from the time he took it over from Hitler in 1929 until its final days. In the hellish complexity of the Nazi state, the Third Reich, all the various hierarchies; Nazi Party members; bureaucrats of the state; the *Wehrmacht* and so on were all infiltrated by the SS, as well as all public and private organisations and commercial and banking institutions. As from 1940 all police functionaries, all the chiefs of the major services and all people of importance to the regime were given honorary SS titles.

Its ideology, formed by Isaac Rosenberg, a philosopher, occultist and author of *The Myth of the Twentieth Century*, increasingly influenced the whole of German life and all positions of management and control were finally absorbed by it. From this ideology came the two fixed basic principles of the SS: racial selection and blind obedience.

Racial selection, although patently a farce, was based on a mix of pseudo-science and ancient German pagan myth, stirred by occult practices. Many Germans privately mocked Dr Goebbels as a misshapen dwarf and, when genealogical researches were being initiated, Hitler personally forbade any investigation into his own Austrian roots. Reinhard Heydrich, head of SS Intelligence under Himmler (and later 'Hangman Heydrich') and one of the most paranoic killers of Jews, was known, by Himmler himself, to have Jewish blood. All these individuals were to play a specific role in some of the events surrounding *Das Reich* in France.

Racial selection theorised that mankind was actually divided between the 'Master Race' and the 'sub-humans'. This sub-

human element was to be totally exterminated. A solemn oath to the Führer committed the SS, and the Gestapo, to the carrying out of the most monstrous crimes without hesitation: the murder of children, women and old people became obligatory. In his speech of 4 October 1943, Himmler reaffirmed this terrible commitment.

The recruitment of the SS 'black aristocracy' was based on precise criteria: to be at least 5' 9" tall (Himmler was 5' 9"), to produce a genealogy going back to 1750, and so on. Out of 100 considered, only ten to fifteen could be selected. The Black Order was destined to represent only five to ten per cent of the total population of conquered Europe, the remainder being relegated to slave status. The SS thus became 'the untouchables' and their entire life was ordered and controlled by Himmler. The dagger awarded to them bore the inscription 'My honour is loyalty' and was a licence to kill with the full awareness of SS protection against such criminal acts. Every SS man was tatooed

SS volunteers take their solemn oath.

Himmler (right) on a saluting base, with Heydrich (first administrator of the concentration camps) to his right, [note the letters 'SD'on his forearm signifying 'Gestapo']. Behind the base is Kaltenbrunner, who took over from Heydrich after his assasination in May 1942.

with his own number, an important check in the post-war identification of SS members accused of war-time atrocities. Most major crimes of the Third Reich were committed by the SS and the Gestapo, all the Auschwitzs and Oradours of the Second World War. The *Waffen SS*, or fighting SS, of which *Das Reich* was a major part, was listed by Himmler as one of the 'five pillars of the SS' at his conference in January 1937.

The Regiment and Its Staff

Against such a background let us now look at *Das Reich* as it appears on the scene in France.

Founded in 1934, it numbered about 20,000 men, equipped with more than 200 tanks: sixty-two Panzer Mark V's of 45 tons each; sixty-four Panzer Mark IV's of 23 tons; hundreds of half-tracks, automatic cannon and tractorised cannon; mortars, flame-throwers and 3,000 vehicles of which 359 were armoured, and 209 heavy tank transporters. Anti-aircraft and anti-tank guns and fifty towed artillery pieces were further supported by Outriders, Reconnaissance, Pioneer, Signals, Medical and other support services.

It is now time to introduce some of the characters involved in this fearsome unit. As to their personalities, in so far as we can understand them, we must start with *Das Reich* Commandant, SS Oberstgruppenführer Heinz Bernard **Lammerding**. Born in Dortmund in 1905 he qualified as a construction engineer in 1932 and, two years later, founded the SS School of Engineering. In 1935 he became SS member number 247062. (In 1929 it had numbered 200). Working in Berlin and Dresden, by 1939 he was responsible for the SS School of Engineering and Strategy and in November of that year became a member of the *Totenkopf* Division. Following the outbreak of war he was involved in closing the Dunkerque pocket around the British Expeditionary Force (BEF) and in 1941 was transferred to the Russian front. Here, and in Prussia, he was responsible, under General von der Bach-Zelewski, for carrying out innumerable massacres as part of the Nazi Anti-Partisan Policy until he took command of *Das Reich* in 1944. His signature is to

SS Oberstgruppenführer Lammerding.

The *Das Reich* Division after its return from Russia in 1944. It is drawn up for inspection by its commander Heinz Lammerding with him is Otto Weidinger, officer commanding *Der Führer*.

be seen on many extermination orders. Awarded the Knight's Cross for his work in Russia, this award was celebrated in Montauban where the Regiment had been relocated.

Following the march north to the battlefront in 1944 he was wounded in the Normandy fighting on 25 July and was later chief of an Army Group on the Vistula under Himmler's command. In 1945 he was hospitalised, arrested by the Americans but liberated after two hours. Following his return to Düsseldorf in July 1945 he was fingerprinted by the British and given his Identity Card. He claimed never to have been in hiding except when the French demanded his extradition when he was advised to go to the mountains to improve his health. Condemned to death *in absentia* in Bordeaux in 1951 for the hangings in Tulle, his extradition was refused by the British authorities. He became a successful businessman and died of cancer at his home in Bavaria in 1971. His funeral in Düsseldorf was attended by 200 ex-SS including Otto Weidinger, a former *Der Führer* commander. In 1969 Lammerding, in company with his former staff officers, Major Albert Stückler and Colonel

Weidinger, granted an interview to two French historians, Georges Beau and Léopold Gaubussen. From his own account he would have seemed to have been a reasonable and modest

man. As to his character, he was not particularly well regarded in *Das Reich* and was evidently a personal friend of Himmler. Administratively able, a good engineer but colourless and of no individual charisma, his abilities seem to have been more pronounced in the field of anti-partisan repression than in fighting against conventional forces.

Major Albert **Stückler** was 1st Staff Officer to Lammerding and was in charge of Operations. A regular *Wehrmacht* officer he was not formally a member of the SS, being on detachment to the Division for organisational and command strategy.

Major Albert Stückler in SS uniform.

Later, immersed in the annihilation battles of the Falaise Pocket in Normandy, he survived and was transferred to the Russian front and very badly wounded in the legs. In 1969, a thin faced and silver haired man, he was only able to walk with the aid of two sticks and needed help in sitting

down and standing up. From his earlier portraits he appears as a lean, intelligent, unyielding person. After the war he remained in close contact with his old SS comrades. As a Staff Officer he seems to have been of a very high quality but he leaves little public aura.

Two lesser figures need introduction here. First, SS Standartenführer Karl **Kreutz** who was responsible for the artillery units. He has been described as being robust and jovial and unlike the stereotyped SS officer. In Russia, too, he had been witness to scenes of unimaginable savagery and merciless retribution. He was to survive the war. SS Sturmbannführer Ernst **Krag**, young and vigorous, was in charge of the

SS Sturmbannführer Krag.

SS Standartenführer Weidinger

assault guns and had been busy at Montauban training up infantrymen to replace his shortage of gunners. His six body wounds served as testimony to the ferocity of his battle experience. He too survived and led a busy life in Germany after the war.

Now we come to SS Standartenführer Otto **Weidinger** who was born in 1914 and joined the SS in 1934. The son of a post office worker, he had been rejected by the army and the police before being accepted by the SS. A passionate athlete, he was immersed in the glamour of SS life and had married early at the age of twenty-four. At the outset of the war he served in the *Deutschland* Regiment and was awarded the Iron Cross in Poland in 1939. Later in France he was again decorated and then participated in the invasion of Yugoslavia and in Operation *Barbarossa*, the attack on the Soviet Union. Further decorations followed while in command of the 4th SS Panzer Grenadiers *Der Führer* in Russia. On moving to France in late 1943 he joined *Das Reich*, survived the march to Normandy, fought in the battles of the Falaise Gap and, later, was part of the spearhead of the Ardennes offensive. At the end, he fought desperate rearguard actions in Hungary, Czechoslovakia and Austria. He was awarded the Oakleaves and Swords at the age of thirty-six.

In the 1960s he participated in the interview granted by Lammerding from which he emerges as a self confident individual with a literary bent. In 1971 he attended Lammerding's funeral and in 1978 published his memoires in a history of the German–Austrian *Der Führer* Regiment, *Comrades to the End*, which makes its fateful contribution to revisionist history. Following his death in 1990 his widow, who describes her husband as a man of great generosity, gave me permission to quote from his book.

Then there are some individuals very closely associated with the major events of the march north. SS Sturmbannführer Helmut **Kämpfe** was Commander of the 3rd Batallion, *Der*

SS Sturmbannführer Kämpfe.

Führer Regiment and a close personal friend of Sturmbannführer Adolf Diekmann who carried out the Oradour atrocity. He was an extremely popular officer and was the most decorated hero of the Division. From his photograph we can envisage him as physically well-built with a strong, characterful face and commanding presence. This officer's disappearance, in the area near St-Leonard-de-Noblat on the night of 9–10 June 1944, is the subject of Chapter 8. Evidence from this event confirms his popularity as his friend, Diekmann, was described as being 'in an agitated state' due to his disappearance. He was physically brave. According to the official German history, Kämpfe was responsible for ordering a French woman, wounded at Guéret, to be taken to the hospital there. From there he is said to have driven to a nearby village to thank the mayor for having repaired a destroyed bridge during the course of the day. Twenty minutes later he was missing.

The Germans claim to have made every effort to obtain his release from the Maquis, even offering to exchange him for thirty Resistance men then held in Limoges. Perhaps negotiations were started.

After the war his widow made contact with the mayor of Cheissoux with a view to retrieving his body. As to his possible burial site, confusion reigns and much of the 'evidence' is based on post war SS disinformation. One such account gives his burial site as Block 1, tomb no. 176 in the German Military Cemetery of Berneuil near Saintes in Charente-Maritime, over 100 miles away: a somewhat unlikely possibility. The most probable site is Cheissoux, at the bottom of a wood near the house of the Delage family, at La Combe de Cheissoux. For further detail on Kämpfe see Chapter 8.

SS Standartenführer Silvester **Stadler** was a member of the HQ Group of the same Regiment. He was the first to receive Resistance gunfire as he drove north when he fell into an ambush at the village of Cressenac. He was a close friend of Kämpfe, who had been his Adjutant in Russia, and was instrumental in initiating the search when news of the disappearance reached him. He is also said to have been the officer who initiated the 'enquiry' into Diekmann's role at Oradour, the result of which was never made public. In 1944 he was transferred to the 9th SS *Hohenstaufen* Panzer Regiment as its Commander and left *Das Reich*.

Of Sturmbannführer Adolf **Diekmann**, the brutal and bloodthirsty Commander of the 1st Batallion, *Der Führer* Regiment, *Das Reich*, relatively little is known. His photograph has yet to be found, no doubt buried amongst the most secret archives of the SS, if it exists at all. Originally a Nazi Socialist Cadet, he was said to have 'a pleasant and infectious laugh'. It was he who was responsible, at Oradour, for the direct implementation of the massacre. Even the account of his death is problematical. He is said to have died in Normandy on 29 June 1944 as a result of imprudently exposing his unprotected head above the parapet of his dug-out. Some accounts attribute this action to suicide. Other accounts claim he survived the war and disappeared. We will meet up with Diekmann when we arrive at Oradour (Chapter 9).

SS Standartenführer Stadler.

Sturmbannführer **Kahn**, 3rd Company Commander, *Der Führer* Regiment, was personally responsible for many murders of French civilians and members of the Resistance, shooting many of them himself. He was No. 2 to Diekmann and issued the orders at Oradour along with Diekmann. It was Kahn who was seen in conversation with Dr Jean Destourteaux at Oradour just before the massacre began. Later, on the Normandy battlefield, he lost an arm, disappeared, and was never seen again.

Finally, we come to Unter-sturmführer **Barth**. At the time of

Oradour he was an 'old SS' NCO. We have his actual words on the road to Oradour: 'You're going to see some blood flow today! And, we'll also find out what the Alsatians are made of'. Condemned to life imprisonment at his trial in East Berlin in 1983, he declared that the events at Oradour were, for him, absolutely run of the mill. His only regret was that he was not allowed to see his grandchildren while in prison. If one can judge from his photograph he would appear to be a low calibre, unthinking individual: 'blind obedience'.

SS NCO Barth.

Lammerding with some officers of *Das Reich* during the period of re-equipping the division in the area of Montauban.

German and Resistance Dispositions Around Montauban

Das Reich was dispersed in some fifty *Lagers* and barracks throughout a fifty miles radius of Montauban. Its triangular area reached to Caylus in the north, Tonneins in the west and Valence-de-Lauragais in the south. It was placed strategically to respond to invasion moves either across the Channel or via the Mediterranean into southern France, and also to help maintain 'peace and order' in the region.

Montauban held no fewer than four large barrack complexes: one near the main station on Avenue Marceau-Hamecher; one to the north of the river on Avenue Bourdeaux; the third near the station Villenouvelle on Avenue

The regimental standard flying between two Pz kpfw Mk V 'Panthers' whilst at Montauban.

du lle Régiment Artillerie. Major Kämpfe's 3rd Armoured Batallion was quartered here. The fourth barrack was Caserne Pomponne on Avenue 19 August 1944. The Regimental HQ was established at Moissac, not in a château as has been reported but in the ancient Collège des Doctraines, now the Trésor Publique, on Boulevard Lakanal, near the Canal.

The 2nd Batallion was located around Castelsarrasin, some three miles to the south of Moissac, and the 1st Batallion *Deutschland*, with the *Der Führer* attached, under Major Diekmann at Valence d'Agen, nine miles to the west of Moissac. Its HQ was probably in the school, Lescipaulou, off the Avenue de Bordeaux. (Every August, Valence presents a spectacle dedicated to the Resistance).

The area is historic: Montauban developed out of a *bastide* of 1144 and is a mellow, red brick town of considerable charm. Its Ingres Museum commemorates one of its most illustrious sons and the church of St Jacques still bears the scars of cannon balls from Louis XIII's artillery siege of 1623. But a more clandestine war was to be opened here in 1944 when French railway

General Inspector of the Panzer Troops Heinz Guderian visited *Das Reich* in May 1944 to observe the Division during manoeuvres.

A burial party conveys a comrade to his grave. SS Sturmmann (lance-corporal) Mahn, *Deutschland* Regiment, was shot during an exchange with elements of the Resistance in the Montauban region, June 1944.

workers began their sabotage attacks on the rolling stock earmarked for use by the Germans. Amongst the earliest saboteurs were two young women who crept into the marshalling yard by night.

As early as February 1944 the Maquis was in action and by 10 May German railway workers were being assassinated in nearby Decazaville. Similar incidents occurred in Capendac, Figeac and Mussidan. Montauban had originally been identified as 'a quiet area' by Field Marshal von Rundstedt (C-in-C Army Group Centre) who had concluded its position would help stabilise communications between Army Groups G and B in the event of Resistance activity worsening throughout France. As Maquis attacks grew, so the 2nd Panzer found itself committed to punitive expeditions into the countryside. Major Stückler later complained, 'We were completely unsuited in character

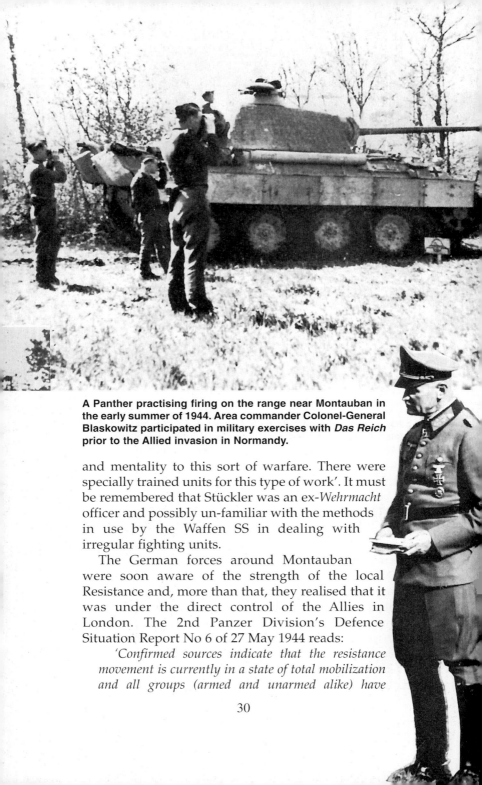

A Panther practising firing on the range near Montauban in the early summer of 1944. Area commander Colonel-General Blaskowitz participated in military exercises with *Das Reich* prior to the Allied invasion in Normandy.

and mentality to this sort of warfare. There were specially trained units for this type of work'. It must be remembered that Stückler was an ex-*Wehrmacht* officer and possibly un-familiar with the methods in use by the Waffen SS in dealing with irregular fighting units.

The German forces around Montauban were soon aware of the strength of the local Resistance and, more than that, they realised that it was under the direct control of the Allies in London. The 2nd Panzer Division's Defence Situation Report No 6 of 27 May 1944 reads:

> '*Confirmed sources indicate that the resistance movement is currently in a state of total mobilization and all groups (armed and unarmed alike) have*

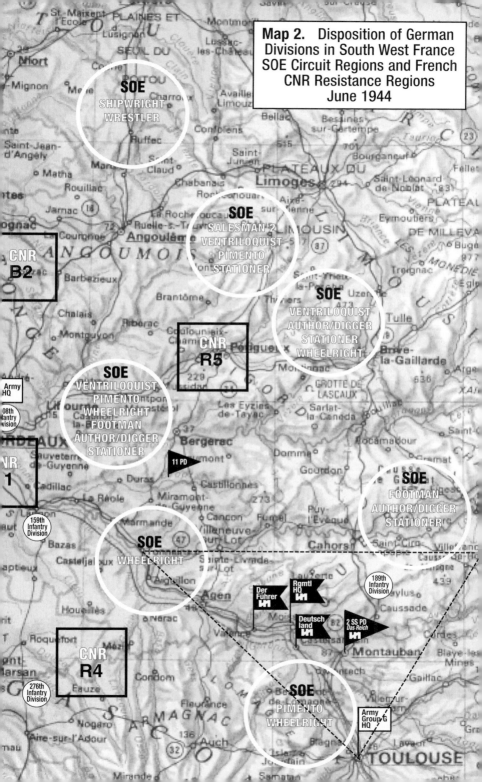

Map 2. Disposition of German Divisions in South West France SOE Circuit Regions and French CNR Resistance Regions June 1944

SOE
SHIPWRIGHT
WRESTLER

SOE
SALESMAN 2
VENTRILOQUIST
PIMENTO
STATIONER

SOE
VENTRILOQUIST
AUTHOR/DIGGER
STATIONER
WHEELRIGHT

CNR
B2

CNR
R5

Army
HQ
08th
Infantry
Division

SOE
VENTRILOQUIST
PIMENTO
WHEELRIGHT
FOOTMAN
AUTHOR/DIGGER
STATIONER

SOE
FOOTMAN
AUTHOR/DIGGER
STATIONER

NR
1

11 PD

159th
Infantry
Division

SOE
WHEELRIGHT

189th
Infantry
Division

Der
Führer

Rgmtl
HQ

Deutsch
land

2 SS PD
Das Reich

CNR
R4

276th
Infantry
Division

SOE
PIMENTO
WHEELRIGHT

Army
Group G
HQ

TOULOUSE

received their operational orders. It is clear that after the start of the invasion the enemy command will drop trained forces in an attempt to take firmer control of the resistance groups and coordinate their efforts with military operations... Regular supply drops by British aircraft supplement the stocks of weapons and ammunition; indeed the entire organisation of the French resistance is almost exclusively in British hands'.

We will familiarise ourselves with the overall Resistance and SOE operation in the Chapter following. In the Defence Situation Report just quoted the Germans also made reference to *'The chiefs, who provide money and arms, live outside the camps . . .'* These chiefs, in the Montauban area, were none other than Tony Brooks (ALPHONSE) and George Starr (HILAIRE) of Special Operations Executive (SOE) whose Circuits, PIMENTO and WHEELWRIGHT, were controlling the region. ALPHONSE was first in the field (1/2 July 1942) parachuting in at Bas Soleil, in the Limousin, and making his way to Lyon, Toulouse, Montauban and elsewhere. HILAIRE had arrived in France on 8 November 1942 on board a Portuguese fishing boat with instructions to work with Circuit DETECTIVE but, as the Circuit had been broken up by the Gestapo, he moved to Agen, in Lot-et-Garonne, and started from scratch. Taken to the village of

Das Reich Regimental HQ, Moissac. The ancient Collège des Doctraines, now Trésor Publique, in 1999.

Castelnau-sous-l'Auvigon, near Condom, he was given effective cover and eventually elected mayor.

Tony Brooks, in an informal chat in 1995, commented on the many inaccuracies in French official histories concerning the Resistance, a criticism I was later to hear repeated by Resistants who had actually participated in the Maquis: parachute operations inaccurately described, Lysanders referred to as bombers, quite frequently the British contribution marginalised. The latter is quite understandable, as far as on-the-ground information is concerned, because SOE security was so tight, not so on the part of an historian. Raymond Aubrac told me that his escape with his wife Lucie from Klaus Barbie, the Lyons Gestapo chief, was 'hardly known about, even by Resistants'. (The Aubrac's amazing story is told in her book *Ils Partiront dans l'Ivresse* and in Claude Berri's film of the same name). Tony Brooks, also in Lyon at that time, was photographed amongst the crowd listening to Marshal Pétain and François Mitterand. After the war Brooks was made Freeman of the city but you will not find his name in the city's Resistance Museum.

Circuit PIMENTO relied extensively on groups of *cheminots*, SNCF railway workers who were prepared to engage in sabotage. The following Chapter, which gives the background to SOE, also details how the Circuits operated with the Resistance. Here we are solely concerned with the events in Montauban itself, in particular with the effect of the BBC message of 5 June 'We will fatten the duck', meaning 'invasion imminent'. Tony Brooks' long laid plans swung immediately into action.

Town Visit

The visitor to Montauban is directed first to the SNCF station on the Avenue Chamier across the Sapiac Bridge. It was here that ALPHONSE's teams went to work, following the intensive training courses he had inaugurated. Using his 'grease-gun' system (whereby abrasives were forced into rolling stock bearings) he disabled the wagons through the carborundum going round and round until it ground up the metal and the axles seized up. Another form of railway sabotage was conducted at the station by means of the signals controller who would start trains moving at the wrong time and so create chaos in the sidings. Rail cuts were effected using British Bickford army fuses which were ignited by a spark from a fog signal cap. French crews would hear this and take the precaution of standing on the opposite side of the

footplate. Electric trains were disabled through the substitution of burnt-out contactors. Bang! When the Germans ran up the driver would shrug and exclaim '*kaput!*' By night, the sabotage teams would be ostensibly checking the good condition of the flat cars and wagons, wielding their 'grease guns' the while. In all, eighty-two tank-carrying wagons, seventy-five steam and twenty-nine electric loco-motives were destroyed and 24 major lines were cut following D-Day. *Das Reich* took to the road.

When at the railway station the visitor should look for two special points of interest. To the station's immediate left a wide gateway leads into a delivery area backing onto the tracks. Climbing onto the raised goods platform one can see the old storage buildings much as they were in 1944. Off to the left can be seen the typical flat-cars which first drew the attention of PIMENTO agents to the fact that such wagons were part of the German pre D-Day build-up. To the right of the station a car park now provides a convenient viewing point of the tracks and target rolling stock.

Oberstgruppenführer Lammerding seen here with Obersturmbannführer Christian Tychsen, who would take over command of *Das Reich* in Normandy, at Montauban shortly before the drive north.

Finally, there is the location of the signals control facility where the head of rail sabotage worked. This has been swept away in the modernisation programme but was located just to the right of the car park. A tablet in the station commemorates the SNCF victims of the Occupation.

Before leaving Montauban the visitor should go to the Museum of the Resistance and Deportation in the Grand Rue Villenouvelle (RM

B-7). Its helpful staff will show you round and it is an essential orientation point for comprehending the Resistance in Tarn-et-Garonne. Amongst its, admittedly limited, SOE exhibits you will see the model of a Lysander, the gift of 161 Squadron, RAF. Your questions will be readily answered and its archives are comprehensive.

Order to Move

Through the effective sabotage of rolling stock at Montauban, the Division had no option but to take to the roads and drive northwards through Resistance-infested countryside to the battles raging in Normandy: a drive of some 450 miles that would put a tremendous strain on engines and caterpillar track links. The repair and maintenance unit, *SS Panzer Instandsetzungs Abteilung 2*, would be kept busy driving its lorries back and forth along the route attending breakdowns. Keeping the troops supplied with fuel and food would be a major operation – a logistical problem that would last over two weeks (the drive should have taken about three days). Coupled with constant attacks and delaying tactics, the tortuous journey would go down in history books as the 'March of *Das Reich*'.

In the early hours of 8 June 1944, the roaring of tank engines, the clatter of tracks and the staccato hail of showers of stones

Selecting routes prior to the drive north: SS Sturmbannführer Kämpfe, SS Sturmbannführer Krag, Colonel Stückler and Oberstgruppenführer Lammerding.

and asphalt announced the departure for the battlefront. Dense blue diesel and petrol fumes billowed up. All over the widely scattered area the Order of March began to shake down.

We now begin to retrace this march north which takes us to the Place de la Libération, along the Avenue 19 Août 1944 and onto the N20, direction Caussade, Cahors and Brive. Ignore the present day rash of billboards and supermarket signs on the outskirts, you are soon in the open countryside which the SS enjoyed in bright summer sunshine with still no intimation of what was to come.

A lengthy rest stop at midday, all proceeded to plan until the afternoon. Some had been sorry to see them go: girl friends had hung garlands on some of the vehicles, but most French were wholeheartedly relieved. By 5 pm the atmosphere began to change. Civilians along the route seemed more reserved. Some villages appeared to be wholly deserted. A peculiar tension hung in the air.

The N20 runs straight as a die beside the railway as far as Caussade. Wheeling through the market square to the left, past the pavement cafés with the occasional astonished and silent customer, *Das Reich* set out along the now twisting N20 to Cahors. Parachute

A pause for refreshment during the journey north, SS Standartenführer Stadler with some of his staff.

drops had been made near here. A short way up the road they passed Montpezat-de-Quercy to the west. How many recalled the 'incident' there on 2 May when, in revenge for a rifle attack on one of the tank battalions, the SS had set fire to several houses, looting others and shooting fifteen civilians? This was part of the *Plan Lammerding* which targeted 5,000 deportees; the requisition of 200 lorries and 400 cars; ten hangings for every German killed; three hangings for every German wounded.

Turn off here onto the D20 and pay a visit to Montpezat and you will be justly rewarded. The glory of this little village is the Collégiate St Martin, the foundation of which dates back to 1159 although there was a church here in 639. Park in the village square, with its lovely timbered houses, the Place de la Résistance. Observe the memorial plaque to a deportee to Ravensbrück, Marie-Antoinette Orcival, 2 May 1944, who died 19 June 1945 in Hamburg. Then, walk down the Rue du Château, past the ancient well head and Lourdes Grotto, and the church of St Martin is in front of you. To the left, the memorial to the villagers killed by the SS; inside, some of the most glorious Flemish tapestries of the 16th century together with splendid treasures of the 14th to 17th centuries. The

Original N20 Montauban to Caussade road runs beside the new road on the left. Route taken by elements of *Das Reich*.

Montauban railway station in 1999 showing flat-cars of the type sabotaged by PIMENTO *cheminots* (railway workers).

excellent guide book available here will enable you to explore six other treasure – house churches in the immediate area.

Moving back up again on the N20 we pass Lablenque, scene of another SOE parachutage (code letter E) organised by George Hiller (MAXIME) and Cyril Watney (EUSTACHE) of Circuit FOOTMAN. Hereabouts the three Circuits PIMENTO, WHEELWRIGHT and FOOTMAN begin to overlap.

Finally, we arrive at Cahors, superbly positioned on the River Lot. The outskirts are as tawdry today as are Montauban's and road traffic can be congested here, particularly on a

Author beside the memorial to hostages killed at Montpezat-de-Quercy.

Montpezat today, church of St Martin is on the right.

Saturday. Nevertheless, Cahors is essential to your trip and you will discover a town of great charm: its famous Pont Valentré bridge is one of the loveliest in France. Romanesque buildings, typically decorated old Quercy houses, balconies and round towers are a joy.

Cahors was the scene of intensive Resistance activity, generated by Circuit FOOTMAN. The German garrison was isolated from all communications when their telephone lines were cut on D-Day. From 6 June the Germans never again ventured outside the town and never repaired their communication lines. The local French Gendarmarie and Police mostly joined the Resistance. Two light aircraft were 'commandeered' at the airfield and on 18 August, after guerilla fighting on the outskirts, the town was liberated and 100 prisoners released. German casualties ran to 207 killed, wounded or captured; the Maquis suffered twenty-seven casualties.

The main port of call in Cahors is the 'Museum of the Resistance, Deportation and Liberation of the Lot'.

Located in the centre of the town, and housed in the old *Caserne Bessières*, it is perhaps one of the most balanced and objective of such museums, fair to many sides of the Resistance and of the contribution made by the SOE and OSS. There are six separate rooms and in the *Salle Jean-Jacques Chapou* many SOE agents are prominently featured. George Hiller's uniform and his parachuted medicine chest should be noted, along with SOE containers, radio sets and the ubiquitous STEN gun (RV Shepherd and HJ Turpin, Royal Ordnance Factory, Enfield, Middlesex). Under the direction of Pierre Combes, the museum staff are enormously helpful and its publications varied and authoritative. They have been awarded the museum Silver Medal by *France* magazine.

The bridge at Cahors during the occupation. Note the barricades.

On 8 June 1944 *Das Reich* traversed Cahors and, on the northern outskirts at St Etienne, divided: the main thrust continued due north, still on the N20, led by Diekmann of the 1st Battalion *Der Führer*; the armour branched east onto the D653 towards Figeac, some elements continuing across the wild and desolate Causse de Gramat (location of several 'safe houses', wireless transmission sites and the scene of

Resistance Museum at Cahors housed in the old barracks.

innumerable parachutages), others continuing along the twisting riverside D662 where they were to encounter a number of ambushes. Our route lies north however and takes us up to the Pont-de-Rhodes over the Céou River where Diekmann's Battalion turned off west through St Charmand on the D704 to Gourdon.

All around them, the Maquis were organising. To the east, on the Causse de Gramat, dramatic events were to unfold, culminating in the 22 July ambush of George Hiller (MAXIME), André Malraux and Marius Loubiéres by German troops armed with deadly dum-dum bullets. To the west, more parachute drops had ensured the Maquis were well armed. Nevertheless, the next five miles to Gourdon remained calm and the lovely old hill top market town, which marks the borders of Quercy and Périgord, rises into view.

Our journey has begun, without incident so far, even if for the tank crews in 1944, the wear and tear on the tracks and the

SOE wireless transmitter being operated at St Laurent-les-Tours, St Céré.

Armed and motorised – Maquis group at a secret camp in the countryside in the summer of 1944.

collapse of connector pins was giving the maintenance personnel a nightmare in the blistering heat of summer.

But, before we arrive at Gourdon and experience the first clash of arms, we must familiarise ourselves with the background of the French Resistance, the nature of Special Operations Executive (SOE) and the situation prevailing in Normandy, the battlefront to which *Das Reich* was called.

A Flammpanzerwagen, Sd Kfz 251, belonging to a unit of *Das Reich*, pictured during the drive north to Normandy.

Circuit: PIMENTO
Dates: July 1942 – August 1944
Principal Departments: HAUTE GARONNE, TARN et GARONNE, DORDOGNE, LOT and CORRÈZE.

Run highly successfully by Tony Brooks (ALPHONSE), the youngest F Section agent ever sent into France, PIMENTO was primarily a sabotage Circuit, wreaking havoc with railway rolling stock through his contacts with the *cheminots* of SNCF thanks to his contacts with CHARLES (later ROBERT) a prominent Trade Unionist. Although much of PIMENTO lies outside *Das Reich* area (notably around Lyon) his 30 'grease-gun' crews and line sabotage operations in Périgueux, Limoges,

Brive, Figeac, Toulouse, Montauban, Agen and Cahors were primarily responsible for forcing *Das Reich* to abandon the railways. As an example, 82 tank-carrying wagons, the property of the *Deutschland* and *Der Führer* Divisions, were destroyed in Montauban in April 1944. Following D-Day, 104 locomotives were destroyed and 24 major line cuts effected by PIMENTO. Important agents in this Circuit were M Mordant (MARTINET); Marcus Bloom (URBAIN); Robert Caza (EMMANUEL), a Canadian.

Tony Brooks holds the DSO and MC.

Tony Brooks.

Circuit: WHEELWRIGHT
Dates: November 1942 – September 1944
Principal Departments: TARN-et-GARONNE, LOT-et-GARONNE, GERS, LOT and DORDOGNE

George Starr (HILAIRE) was the 'unchallenged overlord' of no less than ten Departments. The legend lives on that the Germans believed him to be a British general responsible for the whole of the Resistance in the south west. A 'dead or alive' reward of FF10m was put on his head: no one collected. The history of WHEELWRIGHT is complex: a criss-cross of Gestapo, betrayals, Milice, Jeds, rumours and accusations. Amongst his team: Yvonne Cormeau (ANNETTE) – 'the girl with the golden fingers' – who sent 400 coded messages without a single mistake – see her memorabilia in the Imperial War Museum; Anne-Marie Walters (COLETTE), courier to Starr (known to her as LE PATRON), who

George Starr.

travelled all over an enormous area from the Pyrénées to Périgueux; URBAIN, PIERROT, ARACHAT and many others. Isolating von Blaskowitz's Group C HQ in Toulouse, Starr marched at the head of 1,000 Maquis of the ARMAGNAC Division with Commandant PARISOT and Jed MARK to liberate Toulouse, 21 August 1944. Nine days later, a petulant de Gaulle ordered Starr out of France. Starr stood his ground and was, eventually, awarded the *Croix de Guerre* and *Légion d'Honneur* to add to his DSO and MC.

Yvonne Cormeau.

Circuit: FOOTMAN
Dates: January 1944 – September 1944
Principal Departments: LOT, LOT-et-GARONNE, TARN and HAUTE GARONNE.

George Hiller.

George Hiller (MAXIME) is described as 'diplomatic and cold-blooded'. His Circuit was highly successful and he commanded the deepest respect within the French Resistance. He was charged with 'one of the most delicate missions ever faced by an SOE agent': to locate and close with the elusive Captain VENY, actually Jean Vincent, whose Resistance intentions were unclear in London. Hiller persuaded him to eschew his communist political objective and to fight the common foe. On 14 July 1944, FOOTMAN organised one of the most spectacular parachutages of the war in support of the Resistance. MAXIME had been dropped on 7 January 1944 along with Cyril Watney (EUSTACHE) as Wireless Operator. Other SOE agents: the Mayer brothers (ultimately FIREMAN); Pinder, Cohen, Boiteux and the Americans Blackwell and McCarthy. Very seriously wounded, and close to death, he was rescued by Cyril Watney and operated on in the abandoned presbytery at Magnagues by the light of an old car lamp. A reward, the equivalent of £6,000, was offered for evidence leading to his capture. He was never betrayed. The Verhlacs, Odette Bach and Georges and Odette Bru are among the many Resistants who gave MAXIME unqualified aid.

On returning to England, Hiller received the DSO.

CHAPTER TWO

SOE, SAS AND THE FRENCH RESISTANCE

The Background to SOE

For the visitor to France today, like the SOE agent before him, it is essential to become familiar with the origins of SOE (Special Operations Executive). To do this, two sites are of paramount importance: one located in London, the other near Sandy in Bedfordshire, some forty miles to the north of London and easily accessible by the A1. In London: the Imperial War Museum, Lambeth Road, for the permanent exhibition 'Secret War' which provides the best and most concise overview of SOE.

Here you will find a wealth of original equipment including X-type parachutes; Michelin maps used by agents and Reception Committees; weapons and sabotage equipment; memorabilia including clothing, forged identity papers, photographs and souvenirs of such agents as Yvonne Cormeau and Tony Brooks.

The displays trace SOE's history, its training and operational procedures, RAF and BBC involvement, and the results achieved. You can crawl inside the fuselage of a four-engined Halifax bomber and get some inkling of an agent's experience.

In London, a visit to Westminster Abbey for the SOE Memorial should not be overlooked.

Tempsford Airfield

The site near Sandy and Everton, close by the A1 and just forty miles north of London, is that of Tempsford Airfield from which the majority of SOE agents departed for France on nights of the full moon. Even today a visit to the Dispatch Hut and other old RAF buildings on Gibraltar Farm, set in the lonely, wind-swept farmland, is both evocative and deeply moving. The original barn still stands close to the crumbling runway and a clear path leads from the road directly to it. Inside the barn the poppy wreaths of Remembrance Day and other memorabilia transport the visitor back to those nights in the 1940's when RAF planes took off on clandestine missions with their courageous

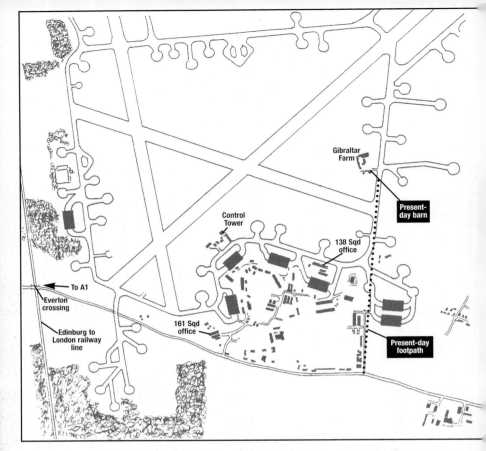

Tempsford Airfield as it appeared during the war years. Over a thousand agents set off for enemy-occupied territory from this secret base from 1942 to 1945.
Gibraltar Farm where agents were supplied with equipment prior to their departure.

The Memorial Barn today captures the atmosphere of the war years. From this building, agents and units who would come up against *Das Reich*, set out on their missions.

TEMPSFORD AIRFIELD
GIBRALTAR FARM

ERECTED TO COMMEMORATE THE BRAVE DEEDS
OF THE MEN AND WOMEN OF EVERY NATIONALITY
WHO FLEW FROM THIS WARTIME AIRFIELD TO THE

FORCES OF THE RESISTANCE

IN FRANCE. NORWAY. HOLLAND.
AND OTHER COUNTRIES
DURING THE YEARS 1942 TO 1945

THE EQUIPMENT FOR THEIR DANGEROUS MISSIONS
WAS ISSUED TO THEM FROM THIS BARN

Tempsford today – some of the huts have survived.
Aircraft types used by the two squadrons, 138 and 161, engaged in
clandestine operations: the Westland Lysander and Halifax Mk II.

cargo of specially trained young men and women headed for the war in the shadows and a destiny fraught with danger and, too often, torture and death.

In Tempsford take a drink in the 'Wheatsheaf' where Kerry and Christine Sabine can brief you on local history. The 'White Hart' is no more but St Peter's church has its SOE memorial and the 'Wheatsheaf' will give you the atmosphere of those days.

There are many other SOE sites in Britain: over fifty primary ones including the several SOE HQs in Baker Street. But now we must come to an understanding of SOE's history.

Some of the memorial plaques attached to saplings close by the Memorial Barn at Tempsford.

ASH TREE IN MEMORY OF
W/CDR.F. YEO-THOMAS
(THE WHITE RABBIT)
WHO LEFT TO UNDERTAKE
CLANDESTINE MISSIONS
IN OCCUPIED FRANCE
FROM R.A.F. TEMPSFORD

BIRCH TREE
PRESENTED
ON BEHALF OF THE
NORWEGIAN RESISTANCE
1987

OAK TREE
PRESENTED
ON BEHALF OF THE
POLISH RESISTANCE
1988

LINDEN TREE
PRESENTED
ON BEHALF OF THE
CZECH RESISTANCE
1989

The History of SOE

SOE was founded by Winston Churchill and derived from the War Council Memorandum of 1 July 1940. Its purpose: 'To set Europe ablaze!' Liddell Hart's *Strategy of Indirect Approach* was to be employed: suddenness, subterfuge and flexibility. From it unfolded a drama almost unparalleled in history.

A red-bordered card in Churchill's 'Hole in the Ground' in Whitehall (ref: INTREPID No B/SOE/1) read:

> *'a reign of terror conducted by specially trained agents, fortified by intelligence, so that the lives of German troops in Occupied Europe be made an intense torment'.*

This unease was to so divert the German commanders, and their collaborators, that it would lead to the loss of a battle, a campaign, the war.

Later, the Americans were to join in. Their equivalent organisation was OSS, the Office of Strategic Services, under the command of 'Wild Bill' Donovan, a close friend of Churchill's INTREPID, Sir William Stephenson, founder of BSC (British

Sir Collin Gubbins

Security Coordination) in New York, himself a friend of President Roosevelt. BSC was a kind of god-parent to both SOE and OSS just as the latter was to be to the CIA (Central Intelligence Agency).

SOE came under the command of Sir Colin Gubbins and its French Section, Section F, under Major Maurice Buckmaster assisted by Vera Atkins, described as 'really the most powerful personality in SOE'. F Section was British (with agents of both British and French origin) and separate from RF Section which was responsible for setting-up cooperation with de Gaulle's Free French forces, although de Gaulle from the start showed little stomach for clandestine warfare.

Recruitment usually began with an individual's meeting with Selwyn Jepson, a man, in Michael Foot's words, 'with a particular talent for this sort of

50

Maurice Buckmaster   **Vera Atkins**

work'. Found acceptable, be they male or female, this was followed by basic commando training and an even stiffer para-military course on the west coast of Scotland.

Demolition work, parachute training, clandestine techniques and security, codes and ciphers, weapons and unarmed combat training were included and, for the wireless operators, wireless techniques, Morse code and set maintenance. Psychological training was based on four premises: an aggressive attitude to work in France; the absolute necessity for patience; indifference to disappointment; and the need for flexibility of thought and opportunist action. Simulated Gestapo interrogations prepared the agent for some of the worst which might befall him or her.

Much of the essential and war-winning attention to detail (French dust in trouser turn-ups, clothes cut by French tailors, etc) was due in no small measure to Vera Atkins, credited by many as 'the brains of the organisation'.

Most agents destined for France were flown by the RAF and parachuted in. Some went by *felluca* (Portuguese sailing ships) or MTBs or MGBs (Motor Torpedo or Motor Gun Boats). SD Squadrons (Special Duties Squadrons) of the RAF (419 Flight, Lysanders; Halifaxes, Wellingtons, Stirlings, Whitleys and Hudsons; and 138 and 161 Squadrons from Tempsford and Tangmere) flew, with the USAF, a total of 7,498 successful sorties.

Reception Committees were organised in advance; landing sites determined; coded signals established and broadcast by the BBC *en clair* – the famous *messages personnels*. On arrival the

Broadcasting coded messages from a BBC studio in London to agents in France.

agent would set up his or her Network (or *réseau*) with its four-fold task of establishing radio communications; arranging the supply of arms, money and sabotage material; finding safe houses; and organising the supply and training of the Resistance. Many agents were also responsible for leading the Maquis into battle and directing the conflict.

A typical F Section team would consist of a leader; a Wireless Operator; and a trained sabotage and weapons instructor. While the men were usually commissioned in one of the armed services, the women were normally commissioned in the FANY (Field Ambulance Nursing Yeomanry) while others held WAAF (Women's Auxiliary Air Force) commissions.

The multiple responsibilities, and complexities of the political scene on the ground, demanded a high degree of diplomacy and *savoir faire*. In the words of the Duke of Wellington: 'The key to victory is the pursuit of all means, however small, which might promote success'. This philosophy was well examplified by SOE.

Operational Plans

Of the many operational plans prepared by SOE perhaps the most successful were *Plan Vert* and *Plan Tortue*. *Plan Vert* (so called because it was typed on green paper) featured maps and drawings prepared by twenty draughtsmen and listed some 800 missions against French railways. Its centrepiece was a series of

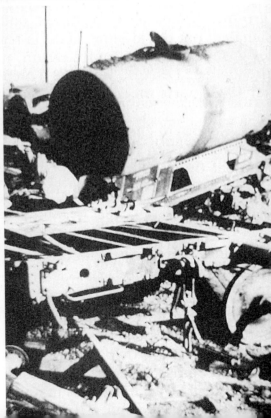

Stages in the kind of destruction brought about by Resistance units to the French rail network.

A blown bridge – one of the many acts of sabotage carried out under *Plan Tortue* which was designed to delay German forces moving northwards.

simultaneous rail cuts designed to prevent designated German units from moving towards the front lines. These rail disruptions were to be maintained while the cross-Channel Allied build-up went forward. *Plan Tortue* (Tortoise) was designed to delay German reinforcements moving up by road by blowing bridges and cutting highways, thus delaying trucks and armour. It contained information for local Resistants on how best to delay Panzer Divisions heading for Normandy by blocking alternative routes, erecting road obstacles, placing mines and creating bottlenecks and ambushes.

Performance and Casualty Rates

At the heart of SOE were the agents themselves, every one a volunteer and fully briefed on the appalling fate which awaited them should they fall into enemy hands. The Nazi policy of *Nacht und Nebel* (Night and Fog) ensured that they would vanish into a hell of anonymous torture and violent death.

Totally accurate statistics on the number of agents sent into France are unavailable. About one quarter of the total number sent into France were from F Section. Maurice Buckmaster gives a figure of 480, a quarter of whom did not return. Of F Section's forty-one women agents over a third did not return. They came from all walks of life and ranged 'from pimps to princesses'. The Jews amongst them ran a double risk. Of all these it was said, 'They loved both France and England and hated the thought of

54

either under Hitler's Germany'.

In material terms, some 10,000 tons of stores and nearly FF 402m in money (new francs) were sent to field agents. Most of the money, all of the wireless sets, all of the aircraft, almost all of the ships, arms and equipment to supply the Resistance throughout France were delivered by SOE.

F Section created about 100 Circuits on French soil. By the Liberation, thirty-one had been eliminated by enemy action; ten had been withdrawn on orders from London; and two had collapsed through internal stresses. On average, an agent's operational life span was about six months.

As to SOE's effectiveness, a wide range of professional opinion gives evidence of its success.

General von Rundstedt in 1944:
> 'all commanders report a general revolt . . . whole formations were simply killed off';

General Eisenhower in 1945:
> 'Special Forces played a very considerable part in our... final victory';

SOE Report No 219/88 of 1944:
> 'The Maquis has inflicted losses... out of all proportion to their own'.

SHAEF Combined Chiefs of Staff Report, 18 July 1945:
> 'Without... SOE "resistance" would have been of no military value';

Maitland Wilson, Supreme Allied Commander, Operation DRAGOON (invasion of the south of France):
> 'the Resistance reduced the fighting efficiency of the Wehrmacht... to 40%'.

William Casey, in Washington in 1982:
> 'The Germans held the French Resistance in much higher regard than did some of our own generals'.

No less a critic, and Resistant, than André Malraux declared:
> 'the general organisation of a plan which made military action possible' was the work of SOE.

While the Resistance came into the open and did battle with the enemy, the SOE necessarily remained more in the background. This Guide should, therefore, throw some light on the war in the shadows.

Seventeen years old FANY volunteer Daphne Marion Walker (assistant to Lieutenant Colonel Musgrove, commander of the JEDS at Milton Hall) with Lieutenant Bob Mundinger of JED TIMOTHY, at the time of their engagement in Piccadilly, London, 1943.

Jedburgh sergeants during a radio practice session at Milton Hall.

As well as the SOE Circuits there were the Jedburgh Teams, uniformed groups of three men, one British, one American, one French, who were dropped behind enemy lines on or after D-Day to liaise with the Maquis and to disrupt enemy forces. American Operational Groups (OGs) operated in much the same way as the Jeds, usually being composed of four officers and some thirty men. Both Jeds and OGs were in action against *Das Reich*. Finally, the Special Air Service (SAS) made its particular contribution to the battle and their BULBASKET Mission forms a separate chapter in this Guide.

Special Operations operatives arriving at Gibraltar Farm, Tempsford prior to take off when darkness falls.

F Section Circuits against *Das Reich*

Circuit	Operational Dates	Time Span
VENTRILOQUIST	May 1941–November 1942 & January–August 1944	27 months
PIMENTO	June 1942–August 1944	26 months
WHEELWRIGHT	November 1942–Sept 1944	23 months
STATIONER	January 1943–March 1944	15 months
SALESMAN 2	April 1943–August 1944	13 months
AUTHOR/DIGGER	September 1943–Oct 1944	14 months
FOOTMAN	January–September 1944	9 months
FIREMAN	March–September 1944	7 months
SHIPWRIGHT	May–September 1944	5 months
WRESTLER	May–October 1944	6 months

Organisation of the French Resistance

In the minds of French veterans, the role of Pétain at Verdun in World War One made him a very respected figure during 1940-1942. However, after Montoire (where he shook hands with Hitler) his popularity declined drastically. 'Resistance' was the virtue of the few and called for unparelleled heroism. Tony Brooks told me that, while the high-ups in the Gendarmerie tended to be collaborationist, the men on the ground were normally OK. A Gallic complexity makes a simple description of the organisation of the French Resistance almost a contradiction in terms. On the one hand an elaborate, structural system was erected in London under de Gaulle, a structure which underwent frequent alterations, additions and revisions. de Gaulle's BCAR (*Bureau Central de Renseignments et d'Action*) was formed in 1942, nearly two years after the inception of SOE.

On the ground, in France, many Resistance groups sprang up spontaneously as from 1940, some of which remained autonomous, as in the case of the Maquis, while others were integrated into a national Resistance organisation, the National

Jean Moulin.

Resistance Council (CNR) in May 1943 under the direction of Jean Moulin, perhaps the greatest of France's Resistance heroes. In addition, a number of secret Resistance groups still remain unknown.

A familiarisation with some of the major French Resistance organisations will help the visitor to appreciate the context of individual actions.

Amongst the earliest on-the-ground organisations were COMBAT; the CONFRÉRIE de NOTRE DAME of Colonel Rémy; LIBÉRATION; and ALLIANCE directed by Marie-Madelaine Fourclade, which developed into ARCHE de NOÉ. Separately, the OCM (*Organisation Civile et Militaire*), FRANCS-TIREURS and the CDLR (*Ceux de la Résistance*) came into being. In the south west, particularly in Périgord and the Limousin, the BRIGADISTES, former Spanish Republicans, and RÉSEAU F2 was formed by Polish officers demobilised in 1940.

The four most important movements were COMBAT,

Maquisards in a forest camp, during the summer of 1944, await orders to move against the Germans.

LIBÉRATION, FRANCS-TIREURS et PARTISANS (FTP) and the ARMÉE SECRÈTE (A/S) under General Delestraint. These were later fused under the title MOUVEMENTS UNIS de la RÉSISTANCE (MUR). In 1944 LA FRANCE LIBRE and the RÉSISTANCE INTÉRIEURE combined, under General Koenig, and became known as the FFI (*Forces Françaises de l'Intérieur*) the A/S having previously formed the ORA (*Organisation de Résistance de l'Armée*) with the FTPF (*Francs-Tireurs et Partisans Français*) controlled by the French Communist Party.

The Maquis, begun in 1941, was not an organisation. It consisted of small, isolated units all over France but particularly in forested or mountainous areas.

Various political and ideological motives drove these different organisations making co-operation difficult and sometimes impossible. This division was largely overcome by the politically neutral British agents of SOE who operated with all of them. Indeed, the British identity was sometimes crucial in saving lives as different resistance groups were, on occasion, known to engage in rival group hostilities. That said, the common cause was always against the same enemy and always for the liberation of France.

German Mountain Troops repair damage to a road bridge as their comrades stand by to provide covering fire should they be attacked by the Maquis.

CHAPTER THREE

NORMANDY INVASION 1944

The greatest sea and airborne invasion ever seen was about to be launched from England onto the coast of France, Operation OVERLORD, D-Day, 6 June 1944.

What German forces were in position to repel the 83,000 British and Canadian and 73,000 American troops who were to land that day?

The German Plan of Defence

Under the direct control of Adolph Hitler was the *Wehrmacht* (under General Keitel), the *Luftwaffe* (under Hermann Göring) and the Navy, the *Kriegsmarine* (under Admiral Karl Dönitz). In the West, in the actual invasion zone, General von Rundstedt was in charge of the Army; Hugo Sperrle of the Air Fleet, *Luftflotte 3*; and Theodor Krancke of the Western Sea Fleet. Army Group B, under Erwin Rommel, was the key. Rommel's HQ was located at La Roche-Guyon, midway between Paris and Rouen.

Superhuman efforts had been devoted to the construction of the Atlantic Wall, a programme largely sabotaged by the Germans themselves when slave construction workers were transferred secretly to work on the V weapon launching sites.

Hitler's *Festung Europa* – coastal fortifications portrayed as an impregnable barrier to any Allied invasion attempt.

Infantry Divisions [716]
Training Divisions (182)
Army Group Boundary —xx—
Army Boundaries —x—

FOLLOW-UP
XXX CORPS
7 ARM° DIV.   49 DIV.
FOLLOW-UP
I CORPS
51 DIV

2 U.S. INF. DIV.
90 U.S. DIV.
XIX U.S. CORPS
LONDON
Thames
VIII BR CORPS
9 U.S. INF. DIV.
XII BR CORPS
II CDN CORPS
V U.S. CORPS
XXX & I BR CORPS
I CORPS
29 U.S. INF. DIV.
VII U.S. CORPS
Severn
AREA Z
ENGLISH
CHANNEL
Cherbourg

347
16 GAF
719
HOLLAND
165
712
19 Pz
148
18 GAF
155 Pz
BRUSSELS
47
331
49
326
(182)
BELGIUM
344
85
245
2 Pz
Somme
17 GAF
348
346
84
FIFTEENTH ARMY
Calais
Scheldt
Mons

319
243
709
91
352
716
711
21 Pz
12 SS Pz
116 Pz
Seine
Marne
PARIS
343
353
266
77
Brest
2 Θ
3 Θ
265
5 Θ
275
Pz Lehr
SEVENTH ARMY
St. Nazaire
Loire
ARMY GROUP B
ARMY GROUP G
Meuse
Moselle

(158)
17 SS P G
708
11 Pz.
FIRST ARMY
F R A N C E
Bordeaux
Loire
Saône
(159)
276
(189)
2 SS Pz
Garonne
9 Pz
NINETEENTH ARMY
(157)
271
277
338
272
Marseilles
244
24?
Rhône

Map 3. Disposition of oposing
forces prior to D-Day
June 1944

A German machine gunner manning a LeMG42 in a 'Tobruk Stand' in the Atlantic Wall defences. Note the grenades at the ready.

Elaborate bunkers (some designed personally by Hitler), the placing of 'Rommel's Asparagus' (anti-landing devices at potential air-landing zones), minefields and the rest were in readiness. But, the outcome depended essentially on man and fire power and the crucial ingredient of morale.

The German mobile Divisions in France contained the best fighting soldiers in the world, and they knew it. The survivors of innumerable successful encounters with British, American and Russian forces, they maintained their high morale, even if the German forces in general contained many second rate elements. They were very largely unaware of the Allied weight of armour and artillery and even less conscious of the Allied Air Force's domination of the *Luftwaffe*. (12,000 aircraft on D-Day compared with the Germans' 300) or of the Navy's ten battleships, thirty cruisers and monitors, three aircraft carriers and eighty-seven destroyers against Germany's three cruisers and a handful of destroyers.

The map shows the distribution of German land forces on the invasion front on D-Day. Army Group B disposed four Panzer Divisions, one of which was Waffen SS, the 12th. 21st Panzer Division was closest to the front while 116 and Panzer Lehr were further back. In addition, seven Infantry Divisions were in position, the closest to the front being 709, 352, 716 and 711. Other units included the 91st Air-Landing Division and the 6th

Parachute Regiment, positioned correctly as it turned out, in the area where the American 82nd and 101st Airborne Units were to fly in. The British 6th Airborne was to come in at Ranville, sandwiched between the German 716 and 711 Infantry Divisions. SS Panzer Divisions numbered about 20,000 men and each Infantry Division about 12,500. Approximately 100,000 German troops were located in the immediate invasion area.

The history of this titanic day is to be found in innumerable accounts and the reader has a wide choice of well researched books to choose from. Our interest lies most particularly in the French Resistance in the area, in the work of the SOE F Section agents and their links with London, and in the various subterfuges designed to confuse the enemy.

French Resistance and SOE

The French Resistance area was called Region M4, with A2 just coming into the picture around Le Havre. In Calvados, the epicentre of the invasion, some 1,500 FFI were mainly concerned with the sabotage of bridges, railway lines and lines of telephone communications. It was in the Manche, towards Cherbourg, that *Plan Vert*, the rail cutting programme, was carried out most spectacularly under Circuit HELMSMAN. Away to the east, in Eure, the maquis *Surcouf* was effective in harassing German reinforcements.

In one sense however, the Resistance here may be said to have been even more effective before the invasion than after. Their Intelligence Services had mapped out every foot of the German defence system from the North Sea to Bordeaux. Marie-Madelaine Fourcade's ALLIANCE had key men in place in the area. One outstanding example: her agent, Jean Sainteny (DRAGON), was handed a fifty-foot rolled up map showing every gun, beach obstacle, all military units and their strengths, and every anticipated landing site, along with all road and rail networks from Dives-sur-Mer to the Cotentin Peninsula. On 16 March 1944, it was picked up by Lysander and flown to London. It was one of the proudest moments in Marie-Madelaine Fourcade's life. The man who had made the map, one Dounin, was caught by the Gestapo, imprisoned in Caen and executed the day after the landings.

The location of every gun was identified by the Resistance. A fisherman named Thomine had noticed that practice shoots by

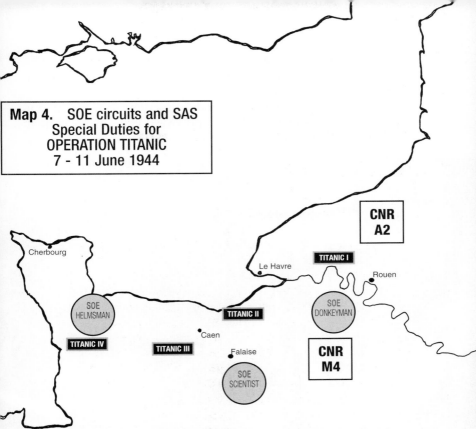

Map 4. SOE circuits and SAS Special Duties for OPERATION TITANIC 7 - 11 June 1944

Cherbourg

Le Havre

Rouen

CNR A2

TITANIC I

SOE HELMSMAN

TITANIC II

SOE DONKEYMAN

Caen

TITANIC IV

TITANIC III

Falaise

CNR M4

SOE SCIENTIST

the Germans were always announced in advance to warn fishing vessels and coastal craft to keep out of the way. By his stealing or copying these notices, and sending them to London, the Allied commanders were fully informed on every coastal gun. A complete Order of Battle was obtained which delineated the strength or weakness of every unit.

The main SOE F Section in place was HELMSMAN run by Jack Hayes. This Circuit was committed especially to the task of collecting tactical information for the American flank. With the aid of thirty local Resistants, who crept through enemy lines, he had accomplished his assignment within a month, much to the satisfaction of the US Army. Circuit SCIENTIST, under de Baissac (DAVID) was engaged in a similar activity a little further south. DONKEYMAN, however, to the east, was to fall foul of double-agents and was betrayed.

In point of fact, the activities of SOE in the Normandy beachhead area did not amount to a great deal. However, two types of signal operations were of crucial importance to the success of the invasion and to the activities of the French Resistance throughout France. First, was the deciphering of the top secret German ENIGMA code, described as 'one of the supreme achievements of the Second World War', by the boffins of Bletchley Park – the ULTRA project – in Britain.

The Sten guns arrive.

Captain JACK (centre) with Colonel Gaucher (right) alias MARTIAL, Departmental Commander of the FFI.

The second was the BBC *messages personnels* sent over in seemingly innocent sounding phrases from London.

The most famous of these was Paul Verlaine's,

Chanson d'Automne: 'Les sanglots longs des violons de l'automne blessent mon coeur d'un langueur monotone...',

the signal that the invasion was imminent. There were many others, triggering off the various Plans: *Vert*, for rail cuts: *Rouge*, for munition dumps; *Noir*, for fuel dumps; *Tortue*, for road cuts; *Bleu*, for electricity lines: *Violet*, for telephone lines; *Jaune*, for enemy communication centres. Hundreds of messages were flashed to France, starting on 1 June with warning, stand-by messages. Then, on 4 June: 'The crocodile is thirsty' – 'Baba calls to Coco' – 'The raven has a red breast' – 'It is hot in Suez' – 'The giraffe has a long neck' . . . The last was for NESTOR, Jacques Poirier of Circuit DIGGER, who received it in company with his radio operator CASIMIR, Ralph Beauclerc, at their Château de la Vitrolle at Limeuil in Dordogne. DIGGER was soon to be engaged in opposing *Das Reich* as it entered his area between Gourdon and Sarlat.

Innumerable deception plans had been laid to confuse the Germans as to the place and timing of the invasion. Of the over 200 German intelligence reports winging into the German 7th Army HQ, only one mentioned Normandy and that had been filed as of 'no consequence'. Rommel was away in Germany and was concentrating on his wife's 50th birthday (Tuesday 6 June).

Much of what the Allies knew of the German reaction to the disinformation provided to them came from ULTRA transcripts. To give just two examples: FORTITUDE NORTH deception plan suggested that six British Divisions were to be landed in Norway; FUSTAG (US 1st Army Group) under the code name FORTITUDE SOUTH suggested that their landings would be in the Pas-de-Calais during July. (ENIGMA picked this up on 9 January 1944). Other diversionary plans included operations such as TITANIC; TAXABLE (deluding the enemy into thinking the invasion would occur north of the Seine); and GLIMMER (a landing near Boulogne).

TITANIC consisted of four separate operations by SAS troops of its 1st and 2nd Regiments allied with French and Belgian units. One example must suffice: TITANIC III. This involved the dropping of fifty dummy (one third scale) paratroopers and 'window', the latter a strip of metal which, dropped in quantities of a few hundred, would reflect as much energy as a Wellington bomber and disturb communications in the area south west of Caen. This occurred at the same time as the 6th Airborne was coming in and while SAS parties were participating in TITANIC I and IV in other locations.

The scene is set.

The effect of *Plan Vert*: Maquisards pose with their handiwork – a derailed locomotive.

CHAPTER FOUR

DAS REICH ENTERS MAQUIS COUNTRY

Adolf Diekmann's 1st Battalion *Der Führer* rolled on through the lovely La Bouraine country, a secretive region of meadows, streams and woods, very little visited and known only to its own local inhabitants. Gourdon lay ahead on the D704. 'Tarry awhile' says the poet Antoine Constanty, 'This is Gourdon, a noble city, calm and smiling, framed by its hillsides'. True still today but hardly applicable to 1944.

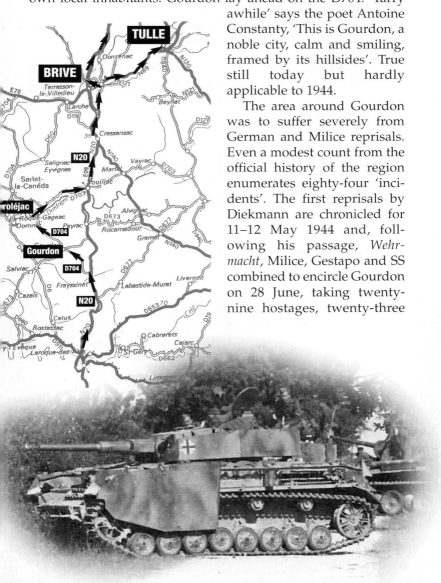

The area around Gourdon was to suffer severely from German and Milice reprisals. Even a modest count from the official history of the region enumerates eighty-four 'incidents'. The first reprisals by Diekmann are chronicled for 11–12 May 1944 and, following his passage, *Wehrmacht*, Milice, Gestapo and SS combined to encircle Gourdon on 28 June, taking twenty-nine hostages, twenty-three

Lot-et-Garonne Resistance Memorial, Lamothe-Cassel, beside the N20.

being shot at Boissiers to the south, and another, René Barrières, being tortured and shot at Lavercantiere, to the south east, on 30 June.

In its official history the 1st Battalion had 'encountered numerous obstacles... and a tiring journey'. It 'had had to engage in several fierce firefights... had suffered its first casualties. Numerous obstacles of felled trees had been removed'. Significantly, Diekmann is described as being in a 'harried and overtaxed' condition.

Here we are increasingly in the region controlled by MAXIME, George Hiller, of Circuit FOOTMAN. Gourdon was linked with Souillac in the Resistance Order of Battle of 8 June. *Armée Secrète*, FTPF, ORA and *Groupes Vény* units were all involved and the names Martin, Grégory, Baudru and Bénech are particularly associated with the Resistance in Gourdon. Amongst the British agents involved with this area (in addition to those already listed in Chapter 2) were the Mayer brothers, Percy and Edmund (BARTHELEMY and MAURICE) of Circuit FIREMAN

Maquisards take up position for an ambush.

French civilians taken as hostages from Gourdon and then murdered as an act of reprisal at Boissiers for the actions of the Resistance.

(which we will meet up with later); the Wireless Operator Paddy O'Sullivan (SIMONET); the Operational Group HELIUM (or EMILY) under 1st Lieutenant Frizzell; and Jed QUININE led by Lieutenant Michel Bourbon (actually Prince Michel de Bourbon Parme, nephew of the Pretender to the throne of France) with Major Tommy Macpherson (ANSELME) and Sergeant Arthur Brown, Wireless Operator (FELECIEN).

We are now in the thick of SOE and Resistance territory and, already, *Das Reich* is beginning to undergo experiences of a kind it had only suffered from before in Russia. A Jed was operating not far from here, Jed ALEXANDER, based on its HQ in the Château de Razac, owned then as it is today, by the de Vigneral family. The present owner told me how, as a girl, she drove the hand-powered generator in the room where their transmitter was installed and recalls how Norman Franklin (who with René

Château de Razac, Dordogne, Jed ALEXANDER HQ.

The tower room from where Norman Franklin transmitted to London.

de la Touche and Stewart Alsop, formed the Jed) would call out, 'Faster! Faster!' to ensure enough power. The room in the château, privately owned of course, remains unchanged since those dramatic days. From its window can be seen the water tower where the Germans installed their observation post which failed to locate the transmitter.

From Gourdon *Das Reich* moved north on the D704: in the first group, the *Der Führer*; in the second, the artillery; in the third, the *Deutschland*. Just after crossing from Lot into Dordogne (and from FOOTMAN into WHEELWRIGHT territory) they came under effective fire for the first time at Groléjac.

The First Resistance Battles

As you enter Groléjac (D704) you will see the Dordogne Departmental panel followed by the sign for the Château de Fénelon. In front of you, is the hillside where the Resistance 'look-out' was posted. He opened fire with a single shot which alerted the village. A Maquis liaison agent, who had been expected, had failed to arrive so they were unprepared although the Jardel Hotel (Hotel du Pont) was full of explosives and the intention had been to mine the bridge.

Continue on until you reach the Casino supermarket on your left. This had been a café at the time and, to the left, you can see the line of the old railway from which the FTP opened fire, bringing *Das Reich* to a halt for the first time.

The D704 approaching Grolejac. Leading elements of the *Der Führer* regiment would have had this view shortly before their first contact with the Resistance who were waiting for them on the approach to the bridge around the corner.

Look-out positioned here, warned of approach

Departement de la DORDOGNE

MkIVs of *Das Reich* at the beginning of the journey through France towards Normandy.

The sole survivor of that engagement today is Maurice Jadel who was fourteen years of age in 1944:

> *The Maquis had driven unexpectedly into the head of the German column and Marcel Malatray, leader of the group was wounded and later died. The driver was killed outright. I was nearby and* Das Reich *officer in command, using impeccable French, ordered me to push the stalled vehicle out of the way.*

The names of the two Maquis members, along with five others, are commemorated on the nearby memorial. (The present memorial is a new one, set up in 1999).

Park your car in the lay-by opposite the Jardel's Hotel du Pont. Walk back and consider the memorial. At the time, the Hotel was in flames,

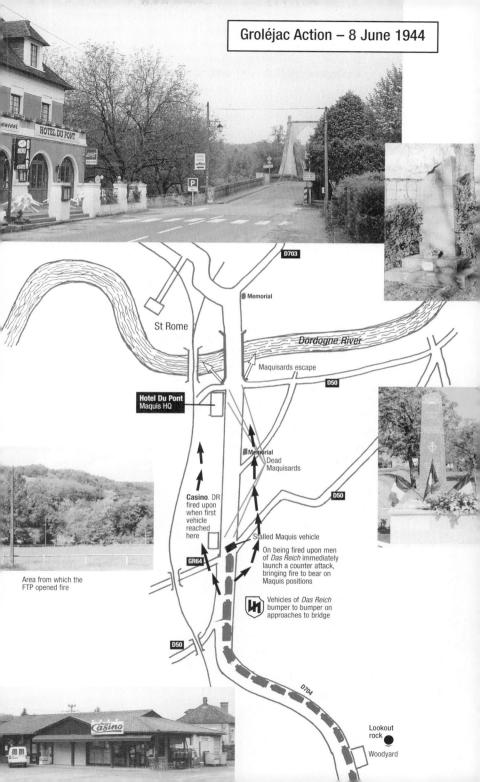

Groléjac Action – 8 June 1944

HOTEL DU PONT

D703

Memorial

St Rome

Dordogne River

Maquisards escape

D50

Hotel Du Pont
Maquis HQ

Memorial
Dead
Maquisards

Casino. DR
fired upon
when first
vehicle
reached
here

Stalled Maquis vehicle

D50

On being fired upon men
of *Das Reich* immediately
launch a counter attack,
bringing fire to bear on
Maquis positions

GR64

Vehicles of *Das Reich*
bumper to bumper on
approaches to bridge

Area from which the
FTP opened fire

D50

D704

Lookout
rock

Woodyard

Casino

struck by a small calibre shell. Five Resistants were shot dead at the little crossroads in front of you and at the entrance of the Hotel – ten died in all.

Maurice Jadel told me how terrified he had been:

I deliberately took my time in pushing the vehicle out of the way. The troop carriers were lined up with their engines running and the steel-helmeted German soldiers were glaring down at me. One of them had his rifle trained on me the whole time. It was an unpleasant experience to look down the barrel of a gun and I knew that if I broke into a run I would be shot in the back. Once I had completed the task, I walked very slowly away until I had turned the corner then I ran and joined the Maquis on the railway line. The tanks and troop-carriers stretched back for at least two kilometers and were an overwhelming sight.

The whole fighting had occupied some twenty minutes and the total delay, some hour or more. No women were killed at

Maurice Jadel at the approaches to the bridge at Groléjac. As a fourteen year old boy he witnessed the fire fight and was ordered by the Germans to push a stalled Maquisard car off the road.

Groléjac at this time but later, when a punitive sweep was made, one woman, sitting at her doorway, was shot dead for her wrist watch. See the second memorial on the north bank of the Dordogne.

You can eat and sleep at the Hotel du Pont, rebuilt after the war by everyone in the commune. Your host will be Bruno Jardel, fourth generation of proprietors. It is located in beautiful countryside, has a fine Romanesque church and is close to François Salignac's famous castle of Fénelon which should be visited.

The columns of fighting vehicles passed over the bridge and *Das Reich* continued on its journey north. Between here and Carsac-Aillac a further thirteen French were to die, including an eighty year old blacksmith. Several houses were set on fire in the hamlets of Bories and Saint Rome. Then the column turned east onto the D703 for Souillac.

Passing through Calviac-en-Périgord and arriving at Rouffillac they were confronted by an enormous barricade. **Stop just before the bridge** where a monument records the names of sixteen civilians killed here along with two Resistants. The incident is a gruesome one: women, children and peasants were taken from the Restaurant Marty, on the opposite side of the road, shot dead by order of Diekmann, and their bodies set on fire with petrol. Miraculously, the next morning, one child of seven years, Irène Paukhialkoof, was found to be alive and was saved.

Roufillac: Memorial to the massacre by the bridge.

The Maquis reported a German motorcyclist killed and an armoured car damaged by bazooka fire. At Carlux two women were shot out of hand at the entrance to the village. At Peyrillac three Resistants died. And so on to Cazoulés and Présignac into Souillac. This had been identified as a Resistance 'hot bed' since, on 6 June, Guedin's Maquis had attacked a German outpost when an armoured train had arrived there. Three Maquis died.

At Souillac we enter FOOTMAN country again. The British War Office Tactical

Vehicles of *Das Reich* made a wrong turning here before returning to the D703 for Aillac.

Investigation of August 1944 reports clashes here on 6 and 7 June and estimates thirty-five Germans may have been killed although official German sources give a total of twelve.

Then, **turn north onto the N20 for Cressenac**. Here the Maquis opened fire on *Der Führer* led by Stadler in a staff car. Several Germans were hit, others leapt from their vehicles in confusion. A heavy exchange of fire followed. Then Wulf and his armour arrived. Cannon and machine-gun fire raked the village and a 75mm shell pierced the church spire. The Maquis lost four and escaped to the east and west. The body of Maurice Vergne was taken away on the bonnet of a half-track to serve as a warning.

Just **north of Cressenac** we enter DIGGER country and immediately afterwards arrive at **Nouailles**. Here a fierce fire fight developed between the 1st Section, C Company, Ace of Hearts Maquis, under Commandant Romain, and Wulf's armour. A three hour delay was imposed on the German column at the cost of several Maquis wounded and some houses burned. Seven Germans were killed. A local *Armée Secrète* chief in the South Dordogne suffered in just such a way from the march of *Das Reich*. His son-in-law now runs a stationery business out of the rebuilt premises of his father-in-law's clothing establishment. (Now Avenue Charles de Gaulle, Terrasson). Informed on locally as a Resistant, the Germans burnt his warehouse to the ground. A railway line that had been cut saw a German armoured train arrive the next day to carry out repairs: two Maquis were killed, one was captured and burnt to death in the furnace of the locomotive.

Jedburg team AMMONIA consisted of Captain Macdonald Austin (USA), Captain Raymond Lecompte (France) and Sergeant Jaco Berlin (USA), radio operator. Landing in a field at Sainte Nathalene, they laid up for two weeks at the farm worked by the Laquieze family where they made contact with EDGAR of Circuit WHEELWRIGHT and the local Resistance chief, M Bararoux (ALBERT). Thereafter they were involved in road cuts on the N20 towards Cahors and line cuts on the Montauban-Bordeaux run and, finally, in fire fights with *Das Reich* on the N89.

Not far from here, on private property at La Pompon, Daglan, can be found the entrance to a secret tunnel, reputedly used by Henry Peulevé in hiding from enemy searches. Local tradition has it that 'the tunnel still belongs to the British Secret Service'!

Max Hastings notes here,

'It was principally the achievements of... SOE officers, together with the Frenchmen they equipped and instructed, which made it impossible to move Das *Reich at any speed. Without SOE, Resistance could have achieved nothing.'*

The report from *Das Reich* to 58th Corps Wehrmacht 10 June, 1944, specified sixty per cent of the tanks and thirty per cent of the half-tracks out-of-service. The lack of petrol was mainly the work of Starr and other SOE agents in WHEELWRIGHT, FOOTMAN and DIGGER.

Only by 7.00 pm did the head of the Regiment reach Brive, there to learn that a *Wehrmacht* Battalion was completely encircled by Resistance forces in Tulle.

Circuit: STATIONER
Dates: January 1943 – March 1944
Principal Departments: DORDOGNE, HAUTE VIENNE, CREUSE, CORRÈZE, ALLIER and LOT.

Maurice Southgate's vast Circuit stretched from Châteauroux in the north, to Tarbes in the south, from Périgueux in the west to Clermont-Ferrand in the east. 'HECTOR needed all his energy and activity for his area was a quite impossible one'. He had parachuted in with his courier, Jacqueline Nearne, a FANY, 'the sensitive dark-haired heroine' of SOE's film *School for Danger*, today the IWM's video *Now it Can be Told*. Southgate's work was so significant that he was gazetted DSO while in the German Concentration Camp from which he was liberated by the

Maurice Southgate (HECTOR)

Americans. Southgate was a pioneer in many respects, notably in the 'blackmail approach' whereby he would present himself to the manager of important factories (Michelin in Clermont-

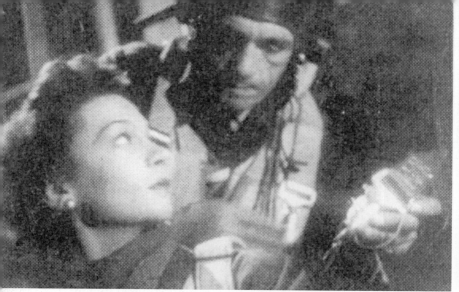

Jaqcueline Nearne gets ready to parachute into France.

Ferrand) and invite the management to sabotage their own works. Refusal was met by Southgate's production of a revolver and the threat of an RAF bomber raid instead. Michelin refused and their plant was demolished by the RAF the very next morning. Peugeot agreed and indulged in self-destruction, a much preferable solution. Pearl Witherington joined HECTOR and, after his arrest, set up WRESTLER. Other agents included STAUNTON (later Circuit SHIPWRIGHT), Mainguard, Shaw, Mattei and the American Milhaud.

Circuit: AUTHOR/DIGGER
Dates: September 1943 – October 1944
Principal Departments: CORRÈZE, LOT and DORDOGNE.

AUTHOR was set up by an English engineer, Henry Peulevé (JEAN) after his remarkable escape from a Spanish prison camp. He made contact with Colonel Vény, and groups of *Armée Secrète* and FTP, and by March 1944 had 2,500 men under his command in Corrèze and Dordogne. Twenty-four parachutages ensured that attacks could be made against German forces and then

80

Henry Peulevé (JEAN)

Jacques Poirier (NESTOR)

Peter Lake (BASIL)

tragedy struck; he was caught with others in a house near Brive and was the only one to return alive from Buchenwald.

JEAN's number-two, Jacques Poirier (NESTOR, also CAPTAIN JACK) took over the Circuit which was renamed DIGGER. In April 1944 he was joined by Ralph Beauclerc (CASMIR) wireless operator, and Peter Lake (BASIL) as his

number two and arms instructor. This successful team was deeply involved with actions against *Das Reich* in Brive, (the first city in France to be entirely liberated by the Resistance) Tulle and elsewhere. They organised more than eighty parachutages including the famous Moustoulat drop of 14 July 1944. In Colonel Gubbins' view this latter saw the 'twilight of Nazi rule not only in Corrèze, but in all of France'. *Das Reich* was attacked on the N20 at Cressenac, Noailles and elsewhere. Jacques Poirier holds the DSO and Légion d'Honneur (Officer).

81

Ralph Beauclerc (CASMIR)

VIOLETTE (René Tallet) leads Dordogne FFI against Milice and Wehrmacht units in DIGGER Circuit country.

Some non-commissioned officers of *Das Reich* in France during the summer of 1944.

CHAPTER FIVE

BRIVE AND TULLE

We arrive at Brive-La-Gaillarde via the N20, turning off by Noailles and entering by the Avenue Edmund Michelet, the same route as that taken by *Das Reich*. Turn left under the railway bridge and head for the SNCF Station (2). This is a good point from which to orientate your visit to Brive, for as the accompanying map shows, most of the SOE and Resistance sites are within easy walking distance. Before coming to the Station, as you enter the town, you will see, to your right, the Grottos of St Anthony of Padua (1). A visit here is very rewarding, not only for the site itself, but for the several tablets commemorating the use of the Grottos as arms caches associated with Henry Peulevé of Circuit AUTHOR.

Your first port of call is *Le Centre National d'Études de la Résistance et de la Déportation Edmund Michelet*, 4 rue Champanatier (3). Located in what was his own home, Edmund Michelet is one of the great heroes of the Resistance. Ten

Grottos of St Anthony of Padua, Brive, site of Peulevé's arms cache.

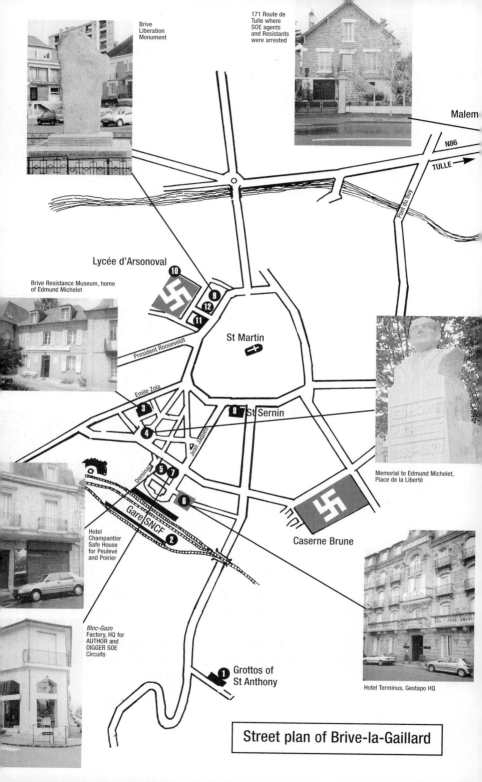

Brive Liberation Monument

171 Route de Tulle where SOE agents and Resistants were arrested

Malem

N86

TULLE →

Pont du Buy

Lycée d'Arsonoval

Brive Resistance Museum, home of Edmund Michelet

10
9
12
11

St Martin

President Rooseveldt

Emile Zola

3

4

8 St Sernin

Jean Jaques

Dominaje

5 **7**

6

Gare SNCF

2

Hotel Champantier Safe House for Peulevé and Poirier

Memorial to Edmund Michelet, Place de la Liberté

Caserne Brune

Bloc-Gazo Factory, HQ for AUTHOR and DIGGER SOE Circuits

1 Grottos of St Anthony

Hotel Terminus, Gestapo HQ

Street plan of Brive-la-Gaillard

exhibition rooms, a library and audio-visual services are served by a helpful and friendly staff including an English-speaking Archivist. References to SOE are mainly on the 2nd and 3rd floors and an excellent map room enables the visitor to visualise the city at the time of the Occupation.

From here the following itinerary is proposed:

1. Walk back to the Station via the Place de la Liberté (4) for the memorial to Edmund Michelet.

2. Turn up the Rue Dumyrat and pass the Hotel Champantier. This was Peulevé's and Poirier's safe house (5).

3. From here, in front of the Station, you have the Hotel Terminus, once Gestapo HQ (6).

4. Then, turn down Avenue Jean Jaures (originally Avenue de la Gare) and at No 26 you have what was Maurice Arnouil's *Bloc-Gazo* factory, the HQ for F Section's AUTHOR and DIGGER Circuits and the scene of innumerable Resistance meetings and events (7).

5. At the bottom of the Avenue you will find the church of St-Sernin where Jacques Poirier attended every Mass one Sunday morning after spending a 'very cold' night in the open countryside and having failed to make immediate contact with Peulevé (8).

6. Moving into the centre, visit the Liberation Monument in Place du 15 August 1944 (9). Across the road the big Lycée building was used to house German garrison troops (10). The nearby Medical Centre saw clandestine operations on wounded Maquis (11) and (12) the home of Dr Lachèze.

Doctor Lachèze, who operated on George Hiller (MAXIME) after his grievous wound from a dum-dum bullet on the Causse de Gramat, worked in this hospital and was responsible for the first 'flying ambulance' to bring medical aid to wounded Resistants. He told me of the first ever arrival of penicillin in France, flown in by SOE to heal MAXIME: its container is still in the Cahors Resistance Museum. See page 44.

Doctor Lachèze

After that, rejoin your car and set out for Tulle, taking the Pont de Buy to the north west of the city and turning east onto the Boulevard President Kennedy and the N89. As you arrive in Malemort, slow down and draw into your right after the Rue M de Vars. You are opposite No 171 Route de Tulle (13).

Few travellers on this busy, dusty road would appreciate the significance of No 171 Route de Tulle. Here, on 21 March 1944, the Gestapo arrested Major Peulevé, Louis Delsanti, the radio operator Louis Bertheau and Roland Malraux, brother of André Malraux, betrayed by a neighbour who suspected them of being black marketeers. They were in course of transmitting to London. After imprisonment in Fresnes and deportation to Germany, only Peulevé returned alive from Buchenwald. It was immediately following this disaster that Captain Poirier took over and set up Circuit DIGGER, the successor to AUTHOR. See page 80.

The monument at Pont de Cornil.

Tulle

From here, continue along the N89, a fast road which twists through increasingly volcanic heights, paralleling the River Corrèze and the railway line. Half way to Tulle, at Pont de Cornil, you will observe a monument on your right. Pull off the road here. The monument records the surrender of Tulle, 16 August 1944, by Captain Reichmann to four

Lieutenant Dennis (Left) holding the German surrender document for the Corrèze with (left to right) Lieutenant Jacquot, a Resistant, Jacques Poirier and Colonel Guedin, at the time of the surrender of Brive.

representatives of the Resistance.

Continue on to Tulle but drive slowly and carefully as the traffic is fast here and you will soon arrive at the *Champ des Martyrs* of the Resistance. A panel will warn you: drive past the site and pull in before the garage on your right. (For visitors leaving Tulle for Brive there is a small lay-by opposite the site but the same caution should be observed and you will have to cross the road on foot). Here the victims of the 9 June 1944 hangings are buried.

Champ des Martyrs, **Tulle, on the N89.**

The memorial reads:
PASSER-BY

–

On the evening of 9 June 1944
in this corner of earth for ever sacred
but which was only a depot
for refuse were ignominiously buried
99 young men savagely
hanged by the SS of Das Reich Division
by order of General Lammerding
To them have been piously brought
some ashes of their 101 comrades
deported and never returning from the Death Camps

–

MEDITATE
REMEMBER

The tragedy of Tulle follows a complex path: where does the whole truth lie? The Maquis attack on Tulle, which began at 5:00 am on 7 June, is detailed on M Dautrement's maps in the Michelet Museum at Brive. It would seem that both French and German sources are more or less in agreement on the initial stages and Max Hastings gives a concise account in his book *Das Reich*. We can only summarise the events which unfolded as Louis Godefoy (RIVIÈRE) and Jean-Jacques Chapou (KLEBER) of the FTP, with their considerable Maquis forces, confronted 750 Germans of the 3rd Battalion, 95th Security Regiment, 500 Milice and innumerable SD and other German units. The battle, however, was unequal in that the Germans were better trained and much more heavily armed. It was, moreover, fighting from a strong defensive position. The techniques of street fighting were little known to the Maquis, most of whom had lived and fought in the woods and hills. By attacking Tulle *before* D-Day, and defying the BBC *messages personnel* and the pleas of the *Armée Secrète*, the attack, in spite

Jean-Jacques Chapou

French peasants, forewarned by FFi Resistance units, flee the imminent arrival of *Das Reich*, June 1944.

The school in Tulle on fire during the heaviest fighting. Viewed from the Military School at Marbet.

of initial success, was doomed. The arrival of *Das Reich* at 9:00 pm on 8 June sounded the death knell for the would-be liberators.

The route you have followed to reach Tulle from Brive is perfect ambush country, but none was made. *Das Reich* reconnaissance unit, under Major Heinrich Wulf, consisted of some 500 men in 100 half-tracks and lorries. They arrived opposite the railway station, switched off their engines and waited. Suddenly, gunfire erupted all around them, triggering a fierce firefight. The FTP lost seventeen killed and twenty-one wounded. The official German report finally listed nine dead and thirty-one wounded of *Das Reich* but a further sixty-two bodies of garrison troops are listed. It was later reported that among the German dead there were signs of mutilation and desecration. However, since mention of this does not appear in the Day's Regimental Report, it is most probably disinformation supplied later so as to go some way to 'justify' the reprisal hangings.

On 9 June, a proclamation was posted throughout the city:

> *Forty German soldiers have been murdered in the most abominable fashion... policemen and gendarmes have made common cause with the communist gangs... forty German soldiers have been murdered... 120 Maquis will be hanged... for the future, three Maquis will be hanged for every soldier wounded, ten for every soldier killed...*

Tulle was to experience the horror of SS reprisal; methods developed in Russia and perpetrated to counter partisan activity and to totally demoralise the civilian population.

For the visitor today it should be emphasised that entry into and circulation within the city is by no means easy. Getting lost myself a helpful policeman said, *'Après la guerre, Monsieur, Tulle était ecrasé!'(After the war Sir, Tulle was flattened).* Roads have been switched, railway tracks torn up, many buildings demolished, enormous new edifices erected, and the work is still going on. The traffic is dense and much of Tulle is on a one-way system. However, it is easy to park near the Museum of the Resistance and Deportation, 2 Quai Edmund-Perrier, near the cathedral. (Map 2, reference points 3 & 4).

The first map of Tulle opposite concentrates on the area associated with the notorious hanging of ninety-nine hostages, ostensibly in reprisal for the reported murder of forty German soldiers but actually part of the SS pacification *Plan Lammerding*. Arriving via the Avenue de Docteur Valette (off the N89) park across the Bridge of the Martyrs (8) in the cul-de-sac Rue Dr Faugeron. From here explore on foot the Memorial (9), the Pont des Martyrs, the Place Faucher (5) and the environs of the *Balcons de Tulle* where the hangings took place. The SS set up their HQ in the Tivoli Restaurant, at that time a quasi-rustic site. The Tivoli name remains (4) but the area is completely redeveloped. The GIAT factory is the site of German resistance against the initial attempt to liberate the town and the

Although not directly involved in the hangings, Christian Tychsen arrived at Tulle 9 June when they were taking place. He would take command of the Division from Lammerding in Normandy. Tychsen was ambushed and killed by the Americans, 28 July, 1944. He was a well liked and respected officer and a post war *Das Reich* veteran's association bore his name.

A death squad of the SS taking reprisals from the civilian populace. This atrocity occurred after the hangings at Tulle. Neither the place nor the SS unit involved is known.

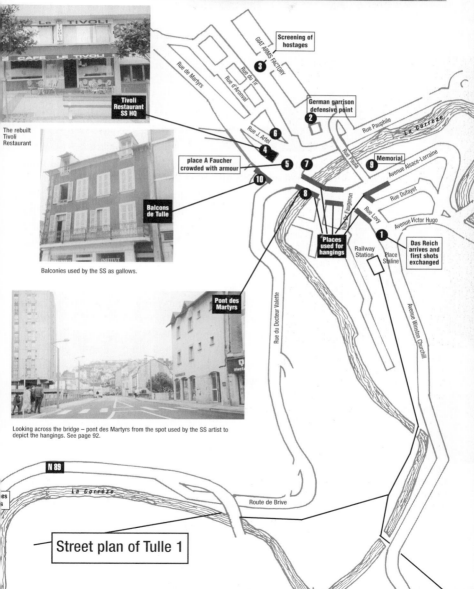

The rebuilt Tivoli Restaurant

Tivoli Restaurant SS HQ

place A Faucher crowded with armour

Balcons de Tulle

Balconies used by the SS as gallows.

Pont des Martyrs

Looking across the bridge – pont des Martyrs from the spot used by the SS artist to depict the hangings. See page 92.

Screening of hostages

German garrison defensive point

Memorial

Places used for hangings

Railway Station

Place Staline

Das Reich arrives and first shots exchanged

GIAT ARMS FACTORY

Rue de Martyrs

Rue du Tir

Rue d'Aromal

Rue J. Artel

Rue Pauphile

La Corrèze

Rue Paula

Avenue Alsace-Lorraine

Rue Dufayet

Rue Ch. Faugeron

Rue Lovy

Avenue Victor Hugo

Rue du Docteur Valette

Avenue Winston Churchill

N 89

La Corrèze

Route de Brive

Street plan of Tulle 1

The cold blooded proceedings at the Tulle road bridge (later named Pont des Martyrs) sketched by an SS officer as they took place.

The much decorated Vincenz Kaiser of the *Der Führer* Regiment took part in the hangings.

School is the one from which the garrison troops surrendered to the FTP (2). The screening of the 'hostages' took place in the factory yard (3); they were assembled at points 6 and 7; the first hangings were at the corner (10) and then across the bridge. Many of the old buildings have gone, some were in course of demolition during my visit in 1999. Here much depends on the visitors' ability to imagine the past but, given the tragic nature of this past, one need not dwell long. Every year the anniversary is commemorated, sprays of flowers being placed on the sites.

Map 2 Tulle. From the Pont des Martyrs drive along the one-way route along the Avenue Victor Hugo and past the Victor Hugo College (2) previously the École Normale which the Maquis captured from the Germans just before the arrival of *Das Reich*. Cross the River at Pont Chisinet and follow the River

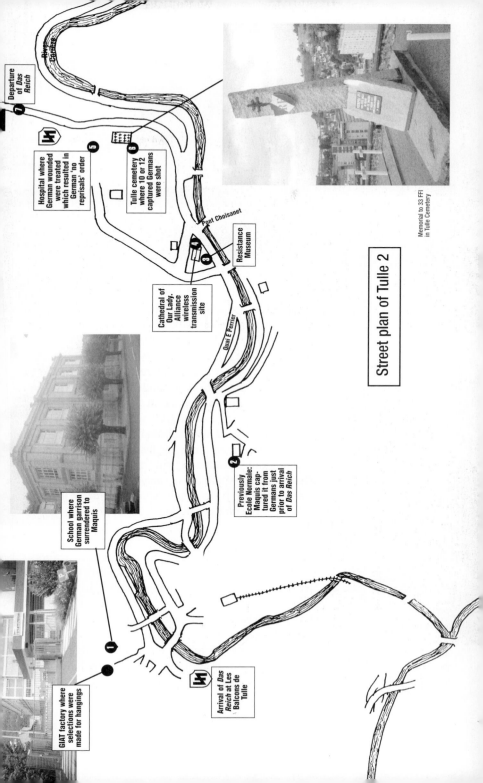

Departure
of *Das
Reich*

River Corrèze

Hospital where
German wounded
were treated
which resulted in
German 'no
reprisals' order

Tulle cemetery
where 10 or 12
captured Germans
were shot

Memorial to 33 FFI
in Tulle Cemetery

Pont Choisanet

Cathedral of
Our Lady.
Alliance
wireless
transmission
site

Resistance
Museum

Quai E Ferrier

Previously
Ecole Normale:
Maquis cap-
tured it from
Germans just
prior to arrival
of *Das Reich*

School where
German garrison
surrendered to
Maquis

GIAT factory where
selections were
made for hangings

Arrival of *Das
Reich* at Les
Balcons de
Tulle

Street plan of Tulle 2

Spays of commemorative flowers on *les balcons de Tulle*, Rue des Martyrs, placed every 9 June.

The Memorial on Avenue Alsace-Lorraine, Tulle.

back on the Quai E Perrier to visit the Resistance Museum (3) and the Cathedral (4) where Circuit ALLIANCE installed their wireless transmitter. Then turn right into Avenue General de Gaulle and pass by the Hospital (5) where the German wounded were treated resulting in a 'no reprisals' order by the German commander. Continue on past the Cemetery (6), where ten to twelve soldiers were said to have been shot, before leaving for Uzerche and Limoges by the N120 (7).

Charles L

In October 1944, after the horror and tragedy of Tulle, the ninety-nine victims were exhumed from their temporary burial site and reburied with full honours at the Champ des Martyrs at Cueille. Also commemorated here are the many deportees who never returned.

Just before we leave Tulle it should be noted that the town contains twenty-eight Resistance memorials and no less than thirty four streets and squares named in honour of its heroes. Some are inside buildings, for example that in the Cathedral to the Abbé Charles Lair who was responsible for the ALLIANCE radio transmitter in the belfry. Several Guide books are available at the Museum detailing these memorials.

As we drive up the N120 for Uzerche we pass through an area which was scattered with *Das Reich* camps at the time and which were inspected by Lammerding who spent the night of 8 June in a flat above a tanner's shop, M Laporte. Here are two memorials to Maquis hanged by order of Lammerding, MICHEL and GERHARD.

From Uzerche you join the N20 for Limoges and continue along it until you approach Le Martoulet near the Forest of Magnac. Here you are entering SALESMAN 2 and VENTRILOQUIST territory and Violette Szabo country. We will now strike off into remote countryside, the details of which route follow in Chapter 6.

Circuit: SALESMAN 2
Dates: April 1943 – August 1944
Principal Department: HAUTE VIENNE.

Philippe Liewer (HAMLET)

After a remarkable clandestine career in Antibes, Périgueux, Mauzac, Rouen and Le Havre, Geoffrey Staunton (Philippe Liewer, HAMLET) parachuted in yet again on 7 June 1944 with Robert Maloubier (PACO), the American wireless operator Guiet and Violette Szabo (LOUISE). HAMLET made contact with Colonel Guingouin, the local FTP leader, with a view to unifying his forces under the FFI banner, as he had been ordered by General Köenig, C-in-C, FFI. Violette Szabo (the subject of Chapter 6) had been a Woolworth's sales assistant, was a complete tom-boy and a deadly shot, described by Vera Atkins as 'incredibly beautiful'. Staunton, with a delegation of four other Allied officers, received the capitulation of Limoges on 21 August 1944 from General Gleininger (see Chapter 7). Staunton was awarded the MC and *Croix de Guerre*.

**Muriel Byck
(VIOLETTE)**

Circuit: VENTRILOQUIST
Dates: May 1941 – November 1942 and March –
August 1944.
Principal Departments: HAUTE VIENNE,
DORDOGNE and CORRÈZE.

We now arrive in Philippe de Crevoisier de Vomécourt's (GAUTHIER) extensive VENTRILOQUIST country, scene of the very first SOE agent landing in France, GEORGE NOBLE on 5 May 1941, and of the first arms parachutage on 13 June 1941. Other agents were to join him: J B E Hayes (sabotage), Dennis Rake (an ex-Ivor Novello singer), Blanche Charlet (CHRISTINE) wireless operator, Muriel Byck (VIOLETTE) a twenty-two year old Jewish girl who succumbed to meningitis and died in Philippe's arms at Romarantin on 23 May 1944. Her name, inscribed on the war memorial there, is one of the very few SOE agents to be commemorated in south west France. Amongst VENTRILOQUIST's many achievements may be noted sixty-five parachutages; more than thirteen bridge blowings; thirty-four German planes destroyed, some in mid-air; thirty ambushes and Maquis battles; along with massive rail cuts. From D-Day on there was no normal rail traffic in this Circuit's area.

GAUTHIER was awarded the DSO, the American DSC, the French and Polish *Croix de Guerre*, the French Medal of the Resistance and was made an Officer of the *Légion d'Honneur*.

Philippe de Vomécourt (GAUTHIER), at a post war parade, receives a decoration from a French General.

CHAPTER SIX

VIOLETTE SZABO

The story of Violette Szabo has been told many times, and rightly so. First in the field was R L Minney's *Carve Her Name with Pride*, originally published in 1956, which became a best seller and is still today a much sought after volume in the secondhand book world. In 1958 a J Arthur Rank film of the same name was made, starring Virginia McKenna, with a screenplay by Lewis Gilbert and Vernon Harris. This chapter concentrates only on those aspects of her work for SOE which are essential for the visitor to the site of her action against *Das Reich* over the period 7 to 10 June 1944.

The Circuit to which Violette Szabo (LOUISE) was assigned as courier that month was the SALESMAN 2 team, commanded by Captain Geoffrey Staunton, real name Philippe Liewer, code name HAMLET. Also in the team was Lieutenant Robert Maloubier (PACO) and an American Radio Operator, Jean Claude Guiet. They were parachuted into France together, on the night 6/7 June.

HAMLET made contact with Colonel Guingouin, the local FTP leader, with a view to unifying his forces with the FFI. In this he was successful and he reported that Guingouin, a controversial figure as a member of the Communist Party and with a sanguinary reputation, 'never failed to execute immediately all orders from London as well as attending to all targets'. As a result of SOE parachutages, Guingouin's FTP was, at the time, about the best equipped Maquis in France. German Intelligence Reports had identified the Limousin area as one of the most dangerous to *Das Reich* in their march north. In his memoires (*Quatre Ans de Lutte sur le sol*

Limousin) Georges Guingouin pays homage to LOUISE's heroism and a brief extract from his book may suffice to give a summary of the last moves in the drama:

'While she and Jacques Dufour (ANASTASIE) were driving to meet a contact near Salon-la-Tour, they ran into a SS ambush. Both armed with machine guns they leapt into a ditch; but they were out-numbered and had to flee across the fields. Unfortunately, Violette fell, twisting her ankle painfully. Strenuously refusing to let her companion help – he wanted to carry her – the English girl bravely told him to save himself. With a superhuman effort, she held out against the pursuers, firing machine-gun bursts at them

Georges Guingouin, *Companion de la Libération*, King's Medal for Courage (King George VI).

while ANASTASIE made a desperate run for safety... Dufour was safe. Violette, however, was taken prisoner and sent to Ravensbrück.'

To this brief account must be added a few words to bring Violette before us. She was twenty-three years of age when she parachuted in that night, a girl of 'haunting beauty', extraordinarily brave from childhood. Already a widow, she left behind a daughter, Tania, born 8 June 1942. Violette was captured two years later, almost to the day, and was to be shot in Ravensbrück seven months later on 26 January 1945.

Let us here take up her story as she climbed, with her three companions, into her US Air Force Liberator on the night of 6/7 June at the secret airfield at Tempsford. Four hours later, after a draught of rum and coffee where they squatted on the floor beside the bomb racks filled with containers of arms and explosives for their mission, they were over the target. Violette was the first to go, dropping through the improvised hole cut in the floor of the aircraft, followed by Staunton, Maloubier and Guiet. Then the plane turned and followed up with their suitcases, guns, ammunition, hand grenades and explosives. The four parachutists swung down to earth.

The Maquis

HAMLET's London briefing had led him to believe that he was to be received by a very well organised Maquis, strictly devoid of political intrigues. They were numerous enough, some 600 and, instead of the expected three members of the Reception Committee, some thirty men came running across the field to greet them. One of the parachutes was caught in the branches of a small wood beside which they had landed. It was quickly freed and the youth who proudly carried it back to the farm is today the proprietor, M Charial of Le Clos. As he was to tell me on my visit: 'We had nothing in those days. The silk was valuable'.

In his report Staunton was to detail how he was dismayed to find that the local chief, Colonel CHARLES, was a saxophonist in a *Bal Musette*, a Private 2nd Class with no war experience. His men were, he reported 'strictly not trained, and commanded by people who had almost decided not to fight the Germans'. He discovered all this on the very night of his arrival. Colonel CHARLES had done the rounds of his billets, revolver in hand, reminding everyone: 'Remember, we are not FTPs'. He was, in fact posing as an Armée Secrète chief in order to ensure that the 'British Imperialists' of SOE would supply the communist Maquis, known as the 1st Brigade of Marche, with all the arms and material they wanted. He need not have bothered. Robert Maloubier was immediately at work, training the Maquis in the techniques of sabotage on the lines of communication. The 1st Brigade was to distinguish itself in later actions.

Parachuting-in

To find Le Clos, you should leave the N20 at the intersection near the Forest of Magnac, half way between Uzerche and Pierre-Buffière, just where the D7 turns off to the east for St Germain. Take the D16 and turn off right for St Vittet and La Croisille-sur-Briance. Then on down the D12 for Surdoux where you turn sharp left for the winding road skirting Mt Gargan, scene of important Resistance battles during the period 11 June to 24 July. Although we are on our way to Violette's parachutage site you should turn aside here and visit the memorial on Mt Gargan

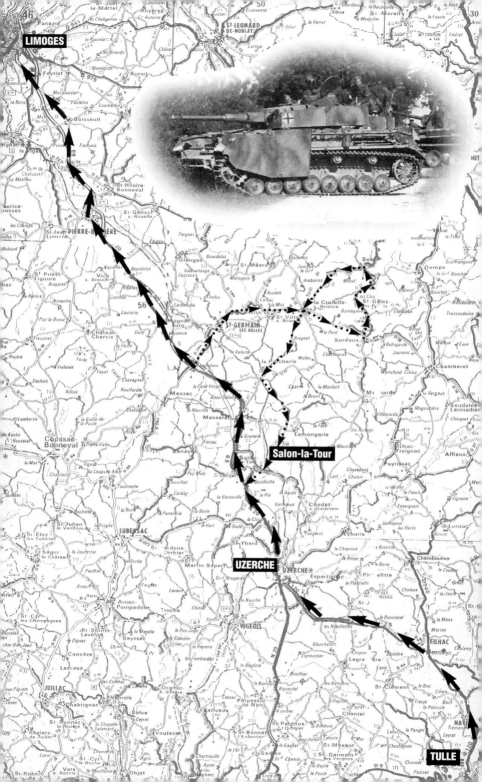

LIMOGES

Salon-la-Tour

UZERCHE

TULLE

commemorating the Maquis loss of 101 to the Germans' 342. Also, the commemoration of the USAF parachutage of 409 containers. In Staunton's citation for decoration he says of Guingouin, 'he was constantly heading counter-attacks and offensive patrols and ambushes. Mastered the situation in the most brilliant way...'

As you wind down to the valley floor you will see Le Clos in front of you. Crossing the stream, away to your right stands a long, low farm and to your left a number of small buildings. M Charial's farm is the last on your left as you begin to mount the hill again. Stop here and look across his fields to the right. In the middle distance you will see a grove of chestnut trees: the exact

Mt Gargan: Resistance Memorial, battle of 17-24 July 1944 with commemoration of 14 July parachutage by B-17s, Flying Fortresses of the USAF.

Le Clos: woodland where the SALESMAN 2 team, made up of four agents, landed on the night of 6/7 June 1944.

The ruined chapel, Mt Gargan.

M Charial points out the grove of trees where Violette Szabo and the three other members of SALESMAN 2 landed.

site of the landing. It was here M. Charial carried the parachutes. 'But, you were only a lad at the time' I said. 'Yes, Monsieur, but they were not very heavy!'

Piling into a large, black Citroen and a lorry brought for the containers, they were soon off. One account gives it that Violette had twisted her ankle on landing. They drove north on the D39 to Sussac. Today you will pass a commemorative panel to the 14 July parachutage of 416 containers as part of Operation CADILLAC and one marking Guingouin's HQ at La Villa. The run to Sussac took them about fifteen minutes and, as they had no fear of a German presence, they laughed and talked excitedly. Had not the Allies just landed on the coast of France? Was not Liberation in the air?

The grocer's shop in Sussac where Mme Ribéras and Mlle Géry welcomed Violette Szabo and the other members of the team.

SOE and Resistants in Sussac: Back row, Mortier (SOE), Fernon, Grelon, Andrew (RAF), Bisset (Jed), Edgar (Jed). Seated, Lannou, Staunton (SOE), de Guelis (SOE), Charles (FTP and A/S) Thomas, Lacoutre.

Arriving in Sussac, drive to the little square in front of the church. Immediately in front of you is the 'safe house' they occupied that night. It is still a general store, its appearance virtually unchanged. Violette had a room to herself, the men shared.

The next morning Staunton called a council of war with Jacques Dufour (ANASTASIE) leader of the local Maquis. Violette was due to make contact with Jacques Poirier of Circuit DIGGER and ANASTASIE offered to take her as far as Pompadour by car to meet up with SAMUEL and so, via a number of contacts, to Poirier's HQ in Dordogne. Staunton emphasised to her the importance of ANASTASIE to his plans for the Resistance in the area: 'Whatever happens, we need him here'. She understood.

Jacques Dufour (ANASTASIE)

On 10 June, at 9:30 in the morning, the little party assembled in the square in front of the church. Violette was dressed in a light suit, flat-heeled shoes and no stockings. She carried her suitcase, Sten gun and eight magazines of ammunition. She also had her bicycle with her. Villagers were struck by her beauty, youthfulness and confident air: she was never forgotten. To a round of good wishes they set off.

We now take the same route, following the D43 to La Croisille-sur-Briance. The road winds and twists through beautiful countryside; it is marked as a 'green route' on the Michelin map. To your left of the road note a new Resistance memorial. At La Croisille they stopped to pick up a friend, Jean Bariaud. Here, if you will and it is convenient, stop for lunch at the Restaurant du Centre for an excellent and inexpensive meal of local specialities. Another Resistance panel marks the centre of the village opposite the restaurant.

Leaving the village take the little D43 road in front of you to La Porcherie, travelling south. In a run of about one hour you will arrive at Salon-la-Tour, passing the lake at Piquette and skirting Lamongerie on the D20E7. You pass under the railway bridge on the outskirts of Salon and the drama is about to unfold.

As you crest the little hill in front of you to your left you will see the old farm buildings exactly as they were in 1944. Ahead, at the end of the road which dips down to the village, you will see the crossroads where the German road-block was erected and from which German soldiers belonging to *Das Reich* waved to the car to slow down. Pull into the right and park next to the rugby football field. Map page 108.

Leaping from their car, ANASTASIE opened fire from the left hand side while Violette leapt to the right and, taking cover from a tree (which is no longer there, an electric pylon having replaced it) opened fire with her Sten gun. Jean Bariaud had

The village of Salon-la-Tour from the east.

Scene of the action.

already taken to his heels. The Germans fired back using rapid fire Schmeissers. They were 400 strong, part of *Das Reich*, making a sweep through the countryside in protection of the main column advancing north to Limoges, or possibly, part of the *Deutschland* 1st Battalion searching for *Sturmbannführer* Kämpfe (see page 24) who had gone missing the night before – accounts vary.

Just down the road to the left (a modern house now stands on the site) a farm woman decided to emerge from her barn, believing that if she remained there the Germans would think she was in hiding and would shoot her. She was cut down instantly. Armoured cars began appearing. Cutting across the road Violette joined ANASTASIE and ran headlong into the farmyard to the left.(2) This is Albert Tisserand's farm today. On 10 June 1944 he was playing in an open barn opposite the farmhouse when he heard running feet and the whizz of bullets, having previously been alerted by the screeching tyres of a car coming suddenly to a stop in the road beside the barn. Leaping the gate into the field, the two fugitives took off across the field towards a small stream. Running into the farmyard, the SS presented a gun to his father and demanded: 'Terrorist or Frenchman?' 'Frenchman' came the reply. 'Setting their machine-gun up on the gate (Albert told me 'It's not *the* gate, it's a new one') they opened fire again', volley after volley pursuing them as they plunged into the ripening corn. Violette received a flesh wound in her left arm. Zig-zagging their way, to avoid leaving a clearly defined trail, they ran up the steep hill towards

Albert Tisserand, right, witness to the Szabo action, explains what he saw.

The gate where the Germans set up their machine gun, firing at Violette and Dufour as they raced across the field heading for the woods.

The bridge where Violette was questioned. Car is in the position of the German half-track. Behind this, at the time, was a pile of logs where Dufour hid, a matter of a couple of metres away from the Germans.

the trees. Suddenly, Violette fell, her ankle twisted. Fighting off ANASTASIE's attempts to pick her up and carry her, she shouted to him to make his getaway. Dragging herself to the edge of the cornfield, she struggled to an apple tree and clamped in another magazine.(3)

Today the apple trees have gone and the cornfield is now a pine plantation. Albert took me to the very site, marked by a young pine of some three feet in height. Here, she stood and fought. Some Germans were seen to fall but by now they numbered hundreds. Finally, her ammunition ran out and, kicking and struggling, she was overcome by two men who dragged her to the top of the hill and down the lane towards the railway. Hot and dishevelled, and in considerable pain, she leant against the parapet of the stone bridge over the railway line.(4) She was not to know, and neither were the Germans, that ANASTASIE lay almost at her feet, hidden under a pile of logs. An armoured car drew up (exactly where the car appears in the photo) and Violette was interrogated by a young officer. Blazing with fury, she rejected his smooth congratulations, spat out his forced cigarette and then spat him in the face. 'All right' he laughed, wiping his face, 'take her away'. 'Tell your men to let go of my arms' she was heard to say as they set off, 'I'll have one of my own cigarettes'. As they passed through the village, the inhabitants peered through their shutters to watch the young English girl go past, her head high. Not many remember now: Albert and a few of his old friends do. Nevertheless, English visitors arrive from time to time and Albert had the honour of a visit by Violette's daughter Tania, who at that time, was living in Australia.

On my visit we turned back to the village, passing the mill on the road Russeau des Forges. There is no memorial to Violette in Salon-la-Tour but a plaque in the square commemorates the execution of Gaston Sarnel of the Armée Secrète by *Das Reich* on 9 June. In the cemetery we went to see the tombs of Jacques Dufour, killed in Indo-China, and of the farm woman who died the day of the gun battle. Further down the track from the stone bridge you can see the railway station where ANASTASIE hid in one of the wagons on escaping from the wood pile. Salon-la-Tour is little changed and it is easy for the visitor to relive the events of fifty years ago. All the surrounding country is as beautiful now as it was that summer day in June. One would like to

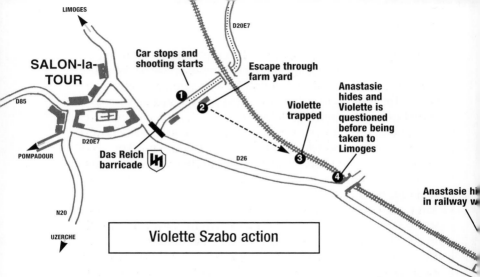

Violette Szabo action

think of that little pine tree growing up to mark, for the future, the last stand of a beautiful and brave English girl who gave her all for France. At Le Clos, on the D39, is the memorial to Violette Szabo unveiled 6 June 2000.

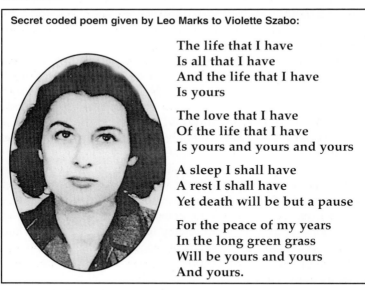

Secret coded poem given by Leo Marks to Violette Szabo:

The life that I have
Is all that I have
And the life that I have
Is yours

The love that I have
Of the life that I have
Is yours and yours and yours

A sleep I shall have
A rest I shall have
Yet death will be but a pause

For the peace of my years
In the long green grass
Will be yours and yours
And yours.

After the Capture

From here, we trace Violette's journey to Limoges which took her to the prison on the Place du Champ de Foire (now the Place Winston Churchill) and to her first Gestapo interrogation at their local HQ. Her interrogator, SS Sturmbannführer Kowatch, had presided the previous day at the hangings at Tulle. Later, she was transferred to the vast Paris prison of Fresnes, to interrogations by SS Sturmbannführer Kieffer (later executed for war crimes) at Gestapo HQ No 84 Avenue Foch. From there she was sent to Ravensbrück, fifty miles north of Berlin, the largest women's prison ever built in the world. Accommodating 7,000 prisoners in 1939 by the time Violette arrived it held over 40,000.

News of the disaster reached Staunton through Jean Bariaud's return to La Croisille late in the afternoon. Setting out to Salon, Staunton was informed that both Violette and Dufour had been taken prisoner, the Germans having put out the rumour that they had captured him as well. However, the next morning two Resistance agents arrived from Limoges with news that an English girl had been brought in the night before, was lodged in the jail and had been seen 'limping badly, but with such dignity...' on her way to questioning at Gestapo headquarters. The Resistance in Limoges was ready to help rescue her. Immediately Staunton and the Resistants evolved a plan. Although it was to be frustrated by her pre-dawn transfer we will follow its manoeuvre when we come to pass some time in the city of Limoges in the next chapter.

There is still talk in Salon-la-Tour about the events of those days. Interestingly, amongst those who remember, the failure of Jacques Dufour to take elementary precautions in driving across enemy infested country is most criticised. Staunton was in little position to do other than use him for the purpose but the French hereabouts contrast the highly trained, valuable SOE agents with their inexperienced, untrained Maquis. Dufour was, they say, far too young for the responsibility he carried, he was in his early twenties. He was too impetuous, a characteristic which could only be put to good use as a result of training. There is evident local regret that the Resistance, at that stage, could not produce what was really required, a reflection which corresponds closely with HAMLET's 'Attachment E' Report on the situation in Haute Vienne just after D-Day. To end on a happier note, he adds:

'I would like to point out that whatever aims the FTPs have for the future, they have for the last three months constantly played the game. I may point out, for instance, that during the last week of August, when Haute Vienne, as well as Creuse and

> *Corrèze were entirely liberated, while both Creuse and Corrèze were sending out about 700 men each to fight in other Departments, Haute Vienne was sending out at the same time over 3,500.'*

When you return to England, pay a visit to the new Violette Szabo Millennium Museum at Cartref, Wormelow, Herefordshire, now the home of Rosemary Rigby. It was here that Violette relaxed between missions during 1944.

Tania Szabo, daughter of Violette, at the unveiling of a memorial to her mother at Le Clos, 6 June 2000.

CHAPTER SEVEN

LIMOGES

Limoges was, to a certain degree, a pro-Pétainist town and his rapturous reception there can be seen on archive film. At the same time it was known as the 'red city' on account of its Communist leanings. In Limoges, arms were successfully hidden in crates of the famous porcelain. Some were not so fortunate for in the same town resident Jews were totally unaware of Vichy's collaboration with the 'Final Solution' – the plan to exterminate all Jews in Europe. The action to round up the victims was taken up more enthusiastically by French anti-Semites than in any other country occupied by Germany. Two memorial plaques on the wall of Limoges prison in Place Winston Churchill commemorate these sad events. Further, Limoges was to be called the 'Capital of the Maquis' by General de Gaulle. It was a dangerous place.

Philippe de la Tour of the *Armée Secrète*, whose fortuitous code name MARIE ANTOINETTE contributed to his survival (the enemy were always looking for a woman) was obliged to attend Partisan 'trials' in his liason role with the FTP. These usually ended with an execution. A former member of the Communist partisans told me of his unease over such proceedings and when asked about the role of the Church he added, 'the parish priests were marvellous'.

Place Wilson, Limoges, 1944. The German garrison in the town was in a state of virtual siege when *Das Reich* arrived.

Another of Philippe de la Tour's responsibilities (he was Reconnaissance Officer) was to sort out the five or six different calibres of ammunition they received: British, American, Spanish, German and so on. It was he who, as a young man, decided to take to the woods and join the Resistance, even though his family objected at that time. Later, they were to see the true colour and worth of this decision.

The German garrison was commanded by General Gleiniger and Limoges had the rare distinction of being fortified with block-houses defended by the GMR. German forces included two Companies of flame-throwers and a Battalion of the 19th SS Police which included fanatical members of the *Hitler Jugend*.

General Gleiniger

As early as 1940 an informal group of Resistants had been formed, sometimes meeting at the Café de Bordeaux. At the same time, Georges Guingouin was setting up his secret force in the Eymoutiers district to the south east. By D-Day the FFI in the area numbered 10,000 men (FTPF, AS and ORA combined). From the SOE standpoint, Limoges was located in SALESMAN 2 country, the Circuit being commanded by Geoffrey Staunton (HAMLET) while, to the west, was Bas Soleil, Philippe de Vomécourt's château, of Circuit VENTRILOQUIST. The SALESMAN 2 assignment parachuted in on 7 June and in subsequent battles and operations played a vital role. Between 25 June and 17 September, seventy-six parachute operations were carried out and a total of 3,695 containers delivered to the Maquis.

Not far from here I met up with Madame T, widow of the local Resistance leader, whose farm had been used as a headquarters. Her village is a microcosm of the Resistance in action and includes the safe house of SOE's radio operator and the house from which he transmitted to London. This house is now lived in by an English couple but until my visit they had no idea of its history. Just behind Madame T's farm is the house where the parachutes, arms and ammunition were hidden. It was here that the Milice made a raid and bullet holes may still be seen in the window frames. Also here is the house where the local parish priest came to the aid of one of the Resistants who was being tortured. Driving out to the parachute sites, Madame T explainedto me:

'I could not speak openly with you in the house, Monsieur, because one of the men present was from a different Resistance unit and we had trouble with them during the war. That is all in the past and we have to live together'.

The villagers still speak with admiration of the skill of the RAF pilots who brought the arms in. The several parachute sites are now markedly different as the trees have grown up and some of the then clear fields have become overgrown.

The last 'messages personnels' broadcast by the BBC included: *Bissou est un bon grandpapa.* Bissou was the Resistant who was being tortured by the Milice until the priest intervened. This Resistant unit, an Armée Secrète Battalion called VIOLETTE, took part in attacks on the *Das Reich* on its way to Limoges. Before I left I was, naturally, treated to one or two glasses of a fine Bordeaux.

Jed ANDY, which operated between July and September 1944 throughout the Limoges, Bellac, St-Leonard, Aixe area of Haute-Vienne, also saw action against *Das Reich* which would send back punitive units even after it had moved north.

Returning to *Das Reich*: the head of the column only reached Limoges at 2.00 am, 9 June, followed by Diekmann's 1st Battalion *Der Führer* at 6:30 am. The main column had arrived by way of the N20 from Brive. All were in a state of near-exhaustion. Immediately upon arrival the officers went to the Hotel de Commandant, the German garrison headquarters, to be briefed on the local situation. The news was not encouraging: the garrison had been cut off from the outside world for two days, no vehicles could get in or out of the city and there were rumours of a Maquis encirclement and imminent attack. Establishing its own HQ in the Hotel Central, the 1st Battalion of *Der Führer* was ordered to St Junien; the 3rd Battalion to St

Leonard-de-Noblat; and the 1st Battalion 'D' to Pierre-Buffière. Reconnaissance and combat missions were also organised, with a view to re-establishing contact with isolated German units and, if necessary, freeing them. All Maquis camps in the area were to be located and destroyed. Sturmbannführer Helmut Kämpfe, commander of the 3rd Battalion, was ordered to lead a patrol to the town of Guéret. Sturmbannführer Diekmann, commander of the 1st Battalion, to St Junien.

Commanders of *Das Reich* confer: Sylvester Stadler, Heinz Lammerding and Otto Weidinger.

When elements of *Das Reich* drove up to Limoges they found a city prepared for attack, barricades blocked off the streets and automatic weapons covered the approaches.

For the visitor, the first port of call is the Resistance Museum by the church of St Etienne. The Museum, under the able direction of M Jacques Valéry (himself a Resistant at the age of fourteen), will enable the visitor to comprehend the complex and multitudinous actions in and around the city, which the tour attempts to summarise. Concerning this Tour, the location of the Pons Garage is no longer certain but may yet come to light. At the Gestapo HQ, after the Liberation, numerous bodies were discovered buried on the site. The Milice HQ was the scene of other appalling tortures. Violette Szabo had been held in the Prison, as had GAUTHIER, Dennis Rake, E M Wilkinson and Richard Heslop, all of SOE. Violette Szabo was interrogated by the Gestapo at their headquarters.

Gestapo HQ in Limoges. Demolished after the war.

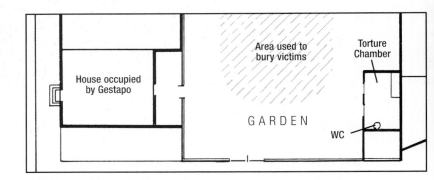

House occupied by Gestapo

Area used to bury victims

Torture Chamber

GARDEN

WC

Out across the river, to the east, can be found the house belonging to M d'Albis, the Swiss Consul, where the surrender terms were negotiated. After quitting Limoges with his 1,500 strong force on 21 August, General Gleiniger 'committed suicide' but it is commonly believed he was either executed, or given a gun for self-execution, by the SS. 'The SS killed everyone', Jacques Valéry reminded me.

The surrender of Limoges was impeccably organised by d'Albis, Guingouin, Staunton (who headed the Allied Delegation), Guery and Viguier of the FFI and Brown of the US Army. With the experience of Tulle behind them, Guingouin refrained from attacking the German garrison with the result that the Allies gained a bloodless victory over the city.

MARIE-ANTIONETTE directs FFI fire in Charente, on the western flank of *Das Reich* march, through the neighbouring Haute Vienne.

Limoges Cemetery, 12 June 1944, a German officer delivers the funeral oration for men of the SS killed by the Maquis at Guerét.

Resistance & SOE Tour of Limoges

The accompanying map provides for a suggested tour of Limoges, taking in the major Resistance and SOE sites. The visitor should start at the Resistance Museum, Henri Chadourne, where a wealth of detail provides the essential background to the overall situation.

1. *Musée de la Résistance du Département de la Haute-Vienne*, Place de L'Evêché.
2. *Restaurant Maupas*, Rue Maupas. Meeting place for Resistants with a back door escape.
3. Approximate position of the *Pons Garage*, Jacques Poirier's safe house owned by Lucien Pons.
4. *Gare Bénédictines*, scene of innumerable Resistant and SOE agent meetings and information transfers.
5. *Impasse St Exupéry*, site of Gestapo HQ, now re-developed.
6. *Rue du Major Staunton*, actually Philippe Liewer, chief of Circuit SALESMAN 2.
7. Corner of *Avenue de la Libération & Rue du General Cerez*, Milice HQ, which even today holds a sinister air.
8. *Prison, Place Winston Churchill*, where Resistants, SOE agents and many other enemies of the Nazis and Vichy were incarcerated. See the commemorative plaques on the wall.
9. *Hôtel Central, Place de la République, Das Reich* HQ.
10. *Hôtel de Commandant, Place Jordan*, German Administrative HQ, now Groupama.
11. *Hôtel de la Paix, Place Jordan*, scene of the capitulation of Limoges by General Gleiniger. Note the Tricolour and Union Jack on the balcony.
12. *Place Wilson*, location of German block-houses.
13. *Rue de St Lazare*, home of M d'Albis, Swiss Consul, where the surrender conditions for Limoges were agreed.

Windows of cells in what was once the Milice HQ, Limoges.

Street plan of Limoges

Limoges Prison where SOE agents and Resistants were held

Limoges Railway Station A significant SOE and Resistants' meeting place

Gare SNCF
Benedictines **4**

5

Champ de Juillet

3

Caserne de la Visitation

6

Avenue de la Libération

Rue Cérez **7**

10

Hotel de Commandant German Administrative HQ

Place Winston Churchill

8

Prison

9 Place de la République

Place Jordan

11

Rue Mauvas **2**

12 Place Wilson

St Etienne

M **1**

Bishop's garden

Vienne

13

Pont Neuf

Milice HQ

SS troops arrive in a French village and begin a 'sweep', an efficient clearance of the houses. This usually meant a search for arms and for the taking of hostages. A terrifying experience for the inhabitants who could have family members shot out of hand.

CHAPTER EIGHT

PRELUDE TO MASSACRE

Three individuals play a decisive role here: the disappearance of Sturmbannführer (Major) Helmut Kämpfe in the hands of the Resistance; the abduction and escape of Obersturmführer (Lieutenant) Karl Gerlach; and Sturmbannführer Adolf Diekmann, with his *Der Führer* Ist Battalion, preparative to the massacre at Oradour.

The Disappearance of Kämpfe

Mention of the disappearance of Kämpfe has been made in Chapter 1. It has engendered a complex history and is one of the most controversial of all the events associated with *Das Reich*. Having sifted through much of the literature, the evidence and the disinformation which abounds, the writer concludes that the following is, in all probability, the closest to the actual truth at the present time.

We can trace the outlines from the official SS history. On 9 June, Helmut Kämpfe was ordered to Guéret with his IIIrd Armoured Battalion in order to liberate the German garrison there which was encircled by the Maquis. Following the action in Guéret, on the evening of 9/10 June, the unit's Medical Officer,

Helmut Kämpfe

Muller, reported 'Kämpfe has fallen into the hands of the terrorists'. He had last seen him at about 8.00 pm when Kämpfe had passed him 'driving alone in his Talbot', had waved vigorously and then accelerated away. Twenty minutes later, Muller was to find the car empty, its engine still running, its doors open, on the road at the edge of a wood. An empty submachine-gun magazine lay under the car. There was no sign of a fight nor traces of blood. The neighbouring woods were combed without result and Muller drove on to report the incident to Command HQ in Limoges. Kämpfe was never seen again by the Germans.

We now pick up the Maquis account. As Kämpfe approached a road junction at the hamlet of La Bussière he slowed down and stopped in response to an on-coming vehicle's flashed

121

Capture of Sturmbannführer Helmut Kämpfe
9 June 1944

SOE VENTRILOQUIST HQ ②

Kämpfe returning from Guéret 8.00 pm

Turned off towards Vernon ④

③

① **Brignac Bridge blown by Canou 7.30 pm**

Interception point at La Bussière 8.30 pm

Kämpfe held at Cheissoux Maquis Camp ⑤

AIGUEPERSE MAQUIS CAMP

VIOLETTE SZABO'S SAFE HOUSE AT SUSSAC

Personnel carrier, Sd Kfz 251 C, belonging to *Das Reich* of the type used in the massacre near Pontarion (D60) after the fighting in Guerét.

headlights. He found himself surrounded by a ring of armed men, Sergeant Jean Canou's FTP.

More local, on-the-ground, information completes the history, enabling the visitor to retrace Kämpfe's movements.

A first-hand oral account was obtained in 1997 by a regional historian, Yves Soulignac, from a neighbour (identified only by the initials JM) who was resident in an old people's home:

> Kämpfe was held prisoner in a Maquis camp near the village of Cheissoux. He had been stopped in his car between 8.30 and 9.00 o'clock in the evening... at the place known as La Bussière between Sauviat and Saint-Leonard [the D941]. He was arrested by the section of Sergeant Canou.'

Although Canou did not enjoy a high reputation for his IQ, and was said to be timid by nature, he was quick to realise the importance of his capture.

More evidence was obtained in 1998 from another witness. Standing at his farmhouse door, wearing clogs as many of the farmers hereabouts still do, MM gave us first hand information concerning the abduction. It was information which did not

The sunken lane at Cheissoux, near the Maquis camp.

surface at the Bordeaux trial, neither has it figured in any of the many histories.

According to this account Kämpfe was preceded by two motor-cycle outriders. They, having passed La Bussière, continued on towards Saint Leonard. A moment later and Canou and his men turned out of La Bussière and, seeing the on-coming Talbot, flashed their lights in a stop signal. Kämpfe stopped and was immediately surrounded. He was unarmed, not even carrying a pistol. He was very relaxed and laughing, fully confident of the immediate arrival of the column behind him and the return of the outriders who would soon make short work of the terrorists. Instead, he was bundled into the lorry and driven off 'up a narrow dirt road'.

For the visitor wishing to retrace these events he should start at the bridge at Brignac, a few kilometers to the north west of Saint Leonard, where the D124 crosses the River Vienne(1).

Canou was returning from blowing this bridge. He drove back to camp by the winding roads used by the locals, travelling north east and actually passing Bas Soleil, Philippe de Vomécourt's château(2). From here the route lay through Lajoumard, Cadillat, past Maisonneuf and then through lanes not now very suitable for traffic to La Vigne and La Bussière(3). At that time the farm here belonged to Pierre Malaquise, who was summarily shot, along with Pierre Mon Just, when they were unable to provide information concerning the whereabouts of the missing officer. Their monument marks the spot. The old farmhouse, which was ransacked, stands just behind the new house, now owned by a Dutchman M van Rooy who was, in his youth, employed by the de Vomécourts at Bas Soleil. (If you appreciate cider you will be well rewarded here).

The lorry carrying the captured SS officer turned down the road marked Vernon(4). This led to the Moulards and Champnétery on the D13 for Cheissoux(5). The Maquis camp was located in the hills at Les Charbonnières. It was in these hills that Kämpfe was held prisoner while news of his important

The road at La Bussière down which Sergeant Canou drove to his head-on meeting with Kämpfe's Talbot. Farm on the left was owned by Pierre Malaquise.

capture was passed to Guingouin at his headquarters.

There is a commemorative monument to the capture of Kämpfe situated further up the D941 towards Bourganeuf, at the bend in the road by Vialleville. Kämpfe was the highest ranking and most decorated SS officer ever to fall into the hands of the Resistance 'the hero of the *Das Reich* Division'and a close friend of Lammerding. On the monument is a quote by General Dwight Eisenhower praising the Resistance for causing a 48-hour delay of *Das Reich* during this period.

Road to Vernon, car in position occupied by Canou's vehicle with captured SS officer Kämpfe.

At the Bordeaux trial in 1953 Canou stated that Kämpfe had been passed over to his chief, Guingouin. One version of later events was that 'he was executed by the maquisards as a consequence of the massacre he had overseen at Guéret'. Other witnesses testify he was shot while trying to escape.

The 'Eisenhower' Resistance memorial at Vialleville.

Without becoming too entangled in the web of mystery surrounding his fate, mention must be made of his supposed grave in the German Military Cemetery of Berneuil, about 100 kilometers north of Bordeaux. Here, tomb No 176, Block 1 bears the inscription: Helmut Kämpfe Stubf 31.7.09 + 10.6.44 Researchers doubt the validity of this inscription.

Perhaps carrying more weight was the convincing testimony of a certain JM interviewed locally:

'Kämpfe was imprisoned, with a German SS officer, in the pigsty of an isolated property situated two kilometres to the south west of Cheissoux. He was executed within 48 hours of his capture after having

The gravestone, in the German Military Cemetery at Berneuil, falsely indicating that Kämpfe's remains are buried there.

> *attempted to escape by digging a trench underneath the door, and was buried in the adjacent copse.'*

A further source confirms that Guingouin ordered his execution upon learning of Kämpfe's responsibility for the massacre at Cambeauvert during the IIIrd Battalion's 'pacification' of Guéret, where thirty-one young maquisards were executed, some by having tracked vehicles run over them.

Below shows the pigsty in which Kämpfe was held but which has subsequently been demolished and replaced by a modern

The pigsty at Cheissoux used as a prison for Kämpfe and his driver, and from where he attempted an escape. It has now been demolished.

A section of the copse at Cheissoux where Kämpfe's body, and that of his driver were probably buried.

addition to the house. Above shows a section of the copse where two Germans were almost certainly buried. However, people living in the vicinity claim to have no knowledge whatsoever as to the precise location. Their main concern seems to be the continued interest of the SS Comrades Association in their possibly retrieving the remains of their former comrade. On this matter the German Embassy also remains silent. The official site of Kämpfe's burial is at Berneuil.

Some of the participants of those days are strongly critical of the activities of the maquisards, even though they tend towards the left politically themselves, and some of them are descendants of Guingouin's FTP: a too hasty urge to kill indiscriminately and to act without due caution. There are criticisms of the fact that the partisans made no attempt to conceal Kämpfe's staff car. Immediately, the Germans were able to pinpoint the exact spot of his abduction, which in turn resulted in sweeps in the vicinity and the shooting of local people out of hand.

Since so much effort was devoted by the SS, at the time and subsequently (even long after the war), to distance themselves from all responsibility for Oradour, the disappearance of Kämpfe (and his subsequent 'reappearance' at Breuilaufa, St Leonard, Limoges and, finally, Berneuil Cemetery) was integral to their plan of disinformation. Further confusion arose with the abduction of Gerlach by the Maquis, another event we must now follow. To do this we must return to Limoges and go out on the N147 to Nieul.

The Gerlach Affair

On 9 June Obersturmführer (Lieutenant) Karl Gerlach (Special Missions Officer) was ordered to reconnoitre billets in the area near Nieul. There are at least two different versions of his experiences. According to his own account, submitted by him to his lawyer on 21 September, 1951, for the Bordeaux trial in 1953, he mentions that he was disappointed with Nieul and moved on to the next town, probably St Gence. Driving ahead rather too quickly he and his driver outdistanced his other two vehicles with their four men. Finding themselves alone they became nervous and turning around they started back towards Limoges, only to find themselves surrounded by maquisards. Stripped of their uniforms they were driven around the countryside in an apparently haphazard way until Gerlach managed to escape near Breuilaufa in the Monts de Blond. Reaching the railway 'after several hours' he struggled down the Bellac-Limoges line and eventually reached the headquarters of *Der Führer* Regiment the next day. He reported

Sylvester Stadler

what had happened to himself and his driver and was promptly ordered to bed by Stadler, his Regimental Commander. Moments later he was awakened by Diekmann, his Battalion Commanding Officer, who demanded a complete description of his adventure.

If the Gerlach affair appears to be a side-play to the tragedy of Oradour its importance lies in the use it was put to by the SS in implicating Oradour as a 'nest of terrorists'. Gerlach claimed, in 1951, to have passed through Oradour as a captive and to have seen there 'maquis and many curious onlookers... numerous uniformed persons, including women wearing yellow leather jackets and steel helmets'. Another version has them in *fauve* jackets, that is fawn colour, a colour closer to the usual GMR uniform (*Groupes Mobile de Réserve*, a para-military Vichy force designed to maintain civil order).

Important also in his statement was his reference to a marker stone inscribed '6.5 Kms to Bellac' near the spot from which he escaped. If this is a true statement it locates his escape point somewhere just north of Blond, on an arc with Virat, some four kilometres to the west of the railway line.

The second version, that of Pascal Maysounave, would seem to place the escape point nearer to Bellac in the Bois du Roi. This route is: Peyrilhac (where he was intercepted by the 4th Regiment FTPF); transferred north to Vaulry in the Monts de Blond; on to Blond itself; then via the D95 and D675 to the Bois du Roi, where he escaped and his driver was shot. From here he reached the railway (about three kilometres) and worked his way back to Limoges.

The incidents in this version are instructive. He was captured and interrogated in Peyrilhac by Madame Marie-Thérèse Pradaud, a German speaking Alsatian. Actually she was not only a sergeant in the FTPF but also a member of the GMR. She, and a group of men, were wearing marine blue uniform and steel helmets while she was armed with a revolver. After

The church at Peyrilhac near the site of Gerlach's capture.

interrogation the two Germans were taken north to Vaulry and on to Blond, where Madame Pradaud lived, and finally to the Bois du Roi. In this version, the group never went into or near Oradour. For this action, Madame Paraud received the *Croix de Guerre avec étoile*.

This route from Peyrilhac to the Bois du Roi takes us through some bucolic countryside, climbs the Monts de Blond, and can easily end up in our becoming lost. It is not surprising that Gerlach found this a confusing route.

Take the D206 out of Peyrilhac, left onto the D101A for Chamborêt.

Gerlach escaped down an avenue of trees in the Forêt des Bois du Roi where this present-day photograph was taken.

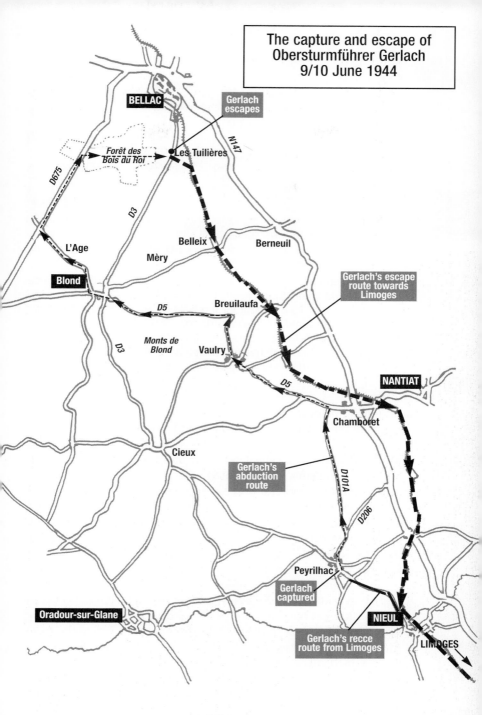

The capture and escape of
Obersturmführer Gerlach
9/10 June 1944

BELLAC

Gerlach
escapes

Les Tuilières

N147

D675

Forêt des
Bois du Roi

D3

L'Age

Belleix

Berneuil

Mèry

Blond

Gerlach's escape
route towards
Limoges

D5

Breuilaufa

D3

Monts de
Blond

Vaulry

D5

NANTIAT

Chamboret

Cieux

Gerlach's
abduction
route

D101A

D206

Peyrilhac

Gerlach
captured

Oradour-sur-Glane

NIEUL

Gerlach's recce
route from Limoges

LIMOGES

131

Hotel de la Gare, St Junien, Diekmann's HQ where the details for the massacre at Oradour were finalised.

Nice, hilly country starts here on the D5 for Vaulry (Resistance memorial) and finally Blond itself. The probable route from here is via L'Age onto the D675 and right for the Bois du Roi. Although the exact site cannot be identified it was certainly along the road through the woods near Les Tuilières, some three kilometres from the railway. This corresponds with Gerlach having passed a 6.5 Kms marker. Return via Belleix and Méry (defaced memorial of 7 August 1944) to Oradour.

We pick Sturmbannführer Adolf Diekmann up again at St Junien, a prosperous leather belt and glove making town on the banks of the River Vienne. He had made the Hotel de la Gare his headquarters on 9 June. With him were Kahn, his No 2; Joachim Kleist, a notorious Gestapo officer from Limoges; an interpreter; and four Milicians. He consulted with the local Gestapo officer, a man named Wickers, and several French officials. The next day he returned to Limoges, 'in an excited state', and conferred over the disappearance of Gerlach, returning to St Junien by noon. After further discussions with Kleist and the Milice he ordered Kahn's Company to mobilise and by 1:30 pm the unit was on its way to Oradour.

But before we follow their movements we must immerse ourselves in an *Armée Secrète* Maquis action which had occurred at St Junien just two days before Diekmann's arrival in the town. As part of Circuit SALESMAN 2's Plan *Vert*, on 7 June the local Maquis had sabotaged the railway viaduct to the west of the town which carried the Limoges to Angoulême main line. The following morning they again took up positions overlooking the viaduct and when the train from Angoulême came to a halt the

The bridge at St Junien from the view of the Germans as they left the stalled train and began crossing the damaged span towards the town where a relief train awaited them. Note, on the right, the balustrade from the original bridge.

passengers were obliged to cross the somewhat perilous spans to join a train which had been sent up from Limoges to meet them. Ten German soldiers were among them: two were shot down, five ran back to the train and three ran forwards to the Limoges train. Those who got back to Limoges reported the incident and the next day an armoured train arrived with a German detachment and Obersturmführer Wickers of the Gestapo. This was but one of literally thousands of similar actions but may serve as an example. The *Armée Secrète* unit had been founded as early as September 1940 and by June 1944 numbered 169 men. On 8 June they followed up the sabotage with the small arms attack described.

Take the D675 south out of St Junien and, after the road bridge, turn right on the D86 for Codille and then first right on an unmarked road until you reach the route de Thonisserie. At the farm at the end of a

The bridge at St Junien today showing the replacement span.

Armée Secrète opened fire from this copse

Span damaged by sabotage

Farm used as operational base by Armée Secrète

muddy track you will see the viaduct and, to your right, the remains of the wood where the Maquis took up their positions. Return to the town and, at the difficult road junction by the chapel (drive with caution), turn left and park near the old glove factories which line the river (Quai des Mégisseries). Climb up and see the ivy-covered piers of the original viaduct with their supports for the old spans. Just away to your left is the wood from which the Maquis opened fire.

We can now set out along the route taken by Diekmann's unit, leaving from the Hotel de Gare which, both outside and inside, is little changed since that day. Although unprepossessing it serves good coffee at a low price. Taking the Avenue travelling east we reach the D32 marked St Brice and Aixe-sur-Vienne. Through St Victurnien, under the new N141, over the old N141, you then traverse the little Rivulet Glanet and mount to Bellevue. Stop. This is the place where the column halted and Diekmann and Barth harangued their men – preparing them for what they would have to do. There is a cross at the side of the road but it is said not to mark any incident associated with the massacre. Climb to the right of the pine trees for a view of Oradour.

The time was 1:30 pm.

Had you been here on 10 June 1944, you would have overheard the chilling words of Lieutenant Barth: 'Today, you're going to see the colour of blood!' Some soldiers were detailed to descend and to begin combing the area in order to conduct anyone they found to Oradour. The bulk of the column moved on down the hill.

View from the bridge at St Junien seen from the position of the men filing across the damaged span.

Armée Secrète opened fire from this copse

CHAPTER NINE

ORADOUR SUR GLANE

Oradour-sur-Glane – a martyred village, a lasting monument to man's inhumanity to man – a sepulchre on the road to Normandy.

Oradour-sur-Glane, in Haute Vienne, some twelve miles to the north west of Limoges. Saturday, 10 June 1944, 2:00 pm. Diekmann established his HQ at the Masset Farm, between Oradour and Les Bordes (D101). Oradour was encircled in a 'classic' SS manoeuvre effectively isolating it entirely from the outside world. Other units traversed the main street, evicting everyone from their houses, places of work and the cafés. Children are evicted from the schools. The entire population was assembled in the Champ de Foire by 2:30 pm. At 3:00 pm the Mayor, M Desourteaux, was ordered to yield up all hidden arms and to provide hostages. Then, the men were separated from the women and children, the latter being taken to the church. 4:00 pm – an explosion, probably a grenade, shattered the peace. Immediately, the SS opened fire; the church was detonated; fires swept through the village. 646 people died. By 7:30 pm much of the village has been consumed by the flames. Later, what remained was sacked and an orgy held in the cellars of the house belonging to M Dupic. On the Sunday, Diekmann's men pulled out of Oradour, loaded with loot and livestock. On

An SS unit moving through the French countryside.

Edit. Villatte

Oradour-sur-Glane as it was before the war and how it appeared in 1944 before the men of the 3rd Company, 1st Battalion, of SS Regiment 4 *Der Führer* of *Das Reich* Division arrived at 8.00 am, 10 June, and began rounding up men, women and children.

Almost certainly this picture includes some of the men who actually took part in the atrocity. This photograph was found at Nieul, near Oradour, and shows men of the *Der Führer* Regiment during Operation 'Zitadelle' on the Eastern Front in July 1943.

the Monday morning, 12 June, the SS returned, dug pits and attempted to leave no further trace of the massacre. They were not successful.

Such are the barest of bones of the frightful massacre at Oradour, the briefest of accounts which leaves out all the horrifying details of one of the worst Nazi crimes committed in France during the Second World War.

Over the years, and at the post-war Bordeaux trial of 1953, many theories have been advanced to explain Oradour to the world. For this writer, the history of the SS (given in Chapter 1) provides the essential key. Recent works (and I would cite here particularly those of Pascal Maysounave, Gérard Guicheteau and David Wingeate Price, see Bibliography) have made it clear that this was no haphazard affair; nothing involving an 'excess of zeal'; no retaliation for Oradour being a 'nest of terrorists' – which it was not, the nearest FTP being 2437 Company located at Villeforceix, some nine kilometers to the north west.

In the official SS historical literature, Oradour is described 'as a reaction to an attack carried out by the French Resistance movement'. That is all. The increasing frustration at the lack of

An unidentified Waffen SS or Wehrmacht unit in action carrying out reprisals against the civilian population.

progress towards Normandy demanded a frightening example and perhaps the timing of the disappearance of Kämpfe provided the trigger for the massacre

This writer believes that Oradour was due to three interlocking factors: one, the SS 'ethic' of elimination, without mercy, of all considered inferior to the Master Race; two, the policy of 'pacification' and reprisal set down in orders of war by the highest German authorities; three, the desperate need to provide a chilling example to the Resistance in the region to bring to an end the harassment of *Das Reich* which was seriously impeding its passage to the life and death struggle for the Third Reich which was being fought out in Normandy.

According to Sturmbannführer Stückler's own memorandum, *Das Reich* had a three-part mission:

1. To maintain liberty of communication 'at any price'.
2. In the event of invasion, to move to the front *ratissant* ('combing') through the widest possible area to eliminate Resistance forces 'so that they would disappear'.

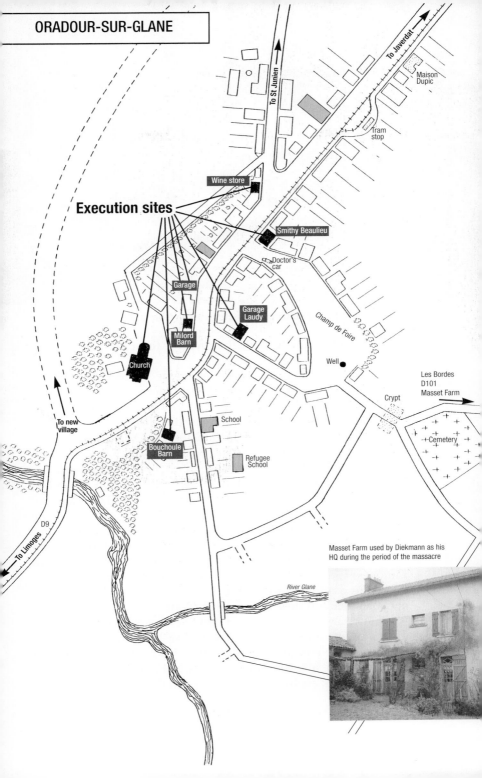

ORADOUR-SUR-GLANE

To St Junien

To Javerdat

Maison Dupic

Tram stop

Wine store

Execution sites

Smithy Beaulieu

Doctor's car

Garage

Garage Laudy

Milord Barn

Champ de Foire

Church

Well

Les Bordes
D101
Masset Farm

Crypt

To new village

School

Cemetery

Bouchoule Barn

Refugee School

D9

To Limoges

River Glane

Masset Farm used by Diekmann as his HQ during the period of the massacre

Charred remains of some of the victims taken from the church and laid out for identification.

3.   To put down 'with the greatest firmness' any civilian aid to the Resistance.

He adds, General Lammerding could be counted on for this mission, his performance in Russia more than adequately illustrating such a capacity.

An increasing number of original documents have come to life which pin-point the responsibility for Oradour very precisely. Amongst them: the strategic German High Command Order of 13 September 1943 (directed at the USSR, Yugoslavia, Greece, Italy and France); 5 June 1944, 2nd Panzer Division *Das Reich* Order No LVIII/120 and Order No LVIII/326 issued 10 June, both issued by Lammerding; and the intervening 8 June Order by von Rundstedt directed to von Blaskowitz. The order of transmission of this Order was: Keitel, von Rundstedt, von Blaskowitz, Krüger, Lammerding, Meier (Chief of Gestapo in Limoges), Stückler, Weidinger, Stadler, Diekmann and Kahn. From these orders derived the concrete plan for the selection, encirclement and destruction of Oradour.

Of special interest is the fact that Diekmann's 1st Battalion at Oradour included a specialist explosives unit. Traces of phosphorus were later found in the church and the unit had been reported, after the war by ex-SS, as having placed twenty-eight anti-tank asphyxiating grenades in the nave.

Having reached the outskirts of the village, descending the D3 to reach the D9, and before we cross the bridge which carries the road, and in 1944 the tramway from Limoges, and before we enter the village itself, let us concretely remember that it was here that 245 women, 207 children and babies and 190 men met their terrible death. Four remained unidentified.

Two hundred SS men of the 3rd Company, 1st Battalion, 4th Regiment *Der Führer* were responsible. In a letter written by General Lammerding for publication after his death he stated that the order for the liquidation of Oradour was given to Diekmann directly by Stadler. There is no mystery about Oradour.

The literature on Oradour is extensive and available at the museum. To guide the visitor, I prefer to quote directly from an actual survivor, Robert Hébras. He takes us, hour by hour, from 8:00 am through to 7:30 pm on Saturday 10 June.

The SS officer directly responsible for the attrocity.

8:00 am	Hébras hears the rumble of heavy vehicles in the street, a rare event. Some German soldiers in combat dress are looking around with an air of indifference. He is not reassured and seeks a hiding place.
1:30 pm	The *Der Führer* convoy stops at Bellevue and then proceeds to Oradour.
2:00 pm	They cross the bridge over the River Oradour and Diekmann establishes his HQ at the Masset farm from where he orders the encirclement of the village. The SS already inside the village get down from their vehicles and start assembling the population. All village exits are closed. The SS show no animosity: it is a simple identity check.
2:15 pm	Everyone is concentrated in the Market Square, babes in arms, just as they are. Anxiety mounts.
2:30 pm	The schools are emptied.
3:00 pm	Men are separated from women. Hébras is disturbed by this development. The women are ordered to walk to the church. The soldiers

A street in Oradour today.
Champ de Foire today. Dr Desourteaux's rusting car can be seen opposite the Smithy.

	speak good French and Hébras does not realise that they are SS. The Mayor is called for and ordered to produce hostages and to turn in all arms. Two sports guns are handed over.
3:30 pm	The men are separated into six groups and directed to different locations in the village. Machine guns are set up. Menace hangs in the air.
4:00 pm	An explosion! The massacre begins. Hébras is wounded and feigns death. Fires are started. Hébras drags himself free and hides. Roofs collapse, yells rent the air and his refuge is set alight. He flees again and takes refuge in a rabbit hutch until that too catches fire at 7:00 pm. He races free.
7:30 pm	Oradour is an inferno. The tram from Limoges arrives. The men are separated from the women, arms are loaded. A second officer arrives and they are told to leave! 'Count yourselves lucky: we have killed everyone here!'

This was translated from the German by Tania Szabo, coincidently, on 11 June 2000. Scrawled across the bottom of the document, in French, are the words: Here is a copy of the brief report from the SS Panzer Grenadier "Der Führer" Regiment concerning the attack of terrorists at Oradour-sur-Glane.   548 dead - French   1 wounded - SS.

SS Panzer Regiment 4   **Reg. Battle Command Post**
      "Der Führer"
              Ia

                              Daily Report for the 10 & 11.6.1944

       SS-Pz-Gren.Regt.4 "Der Führer" extended cleaning-up action on 10 &
       11.6.1944 in the surrounding area.

           1/SS DF   fell on **ORADOUR** on 10.6.1944 and surrounded the place.
                         After a search of the place this was burnt to the ground.
                         Munitions were stored in practically every house.

                         On 11.6.1944, 14.50 hrs 2 communists escaped from
                         NIEUL to **CHATEAUX**. The terrorists had already left
                         the place during the night of 10 - 11 June.

                         Results:
                         548 enemy dead
                         -/1/1 single wounded

           F.d.R.d.A
           (signed)
           Officer

Oradour

This is the grim carcase
of a slaughtered town
its bones picked bare
by history,
silent but for those,
their ashes uninterred,
who haunt the empty streets
and seek the solace of the grave
The rest is the silent echo
of the guns and flames
that burst so vilely on their world
that summer afternoon
and the ruins
and the death.
No hope, no forgiveness
not even vengeance,
just death made formal
by the litany
of the names
of the dead
on marble slabs
and a small, sad casket
of ash and bone
that is all that is left
of those who died.

Richard Davies

CHAPTER TEN

OPERATION BULBASKET AND THE 'JEDS'

Operation BULBASKET was a Special Air Service action, launched at the time of TITANIC and other SAS actions already discussed in Chapter 3. The SAS were required to co-operate with SOE actions and very largely did so.

The SAS was born in the Western Desert in 1941, the concept of David Sterling. Here it had created havoc and mayhem in enemy held rear areas. SAS, and Sterling himself, quickly became something of a legend and in 1944 they were brought back to England to participate in the invasion of France. Training took place in Ayrshire and the 1st and 2nd SAS Regiments trained alongside their French equivalents. In all, about 2,000 SAS men operated in France.

The 7 October 1942, German Armed Forces report, was extended by Hitler in his *Kommandobefehl* Order of 18 October 1942, so that 'all... so-called Commando missions... even if they are to all appearances soldiers in uniform... whether armed or unarmed... are to be slaughtered to the last man... No pardon is to be granted to them...' This order was to have its inevitable consequences for BULBASKET. Indeed, of the one hundred SAS

A Stirling bomber, probably from Tempsford, dropping supplies at night to operatives in northern France.

men captured by the Germans only four survived.

The effective, but tragic, BULBASKET Mission and the march north of the *Das Reich* constitutes the last action site in this Guide.

Action Summary

Landing by parachute on 6 June south west of Châteauroux (Captain Tonkin and Lieutenant Crisp near St-Gautier; Lieutenant Stephens and his main recce party at Bouesse) they were to be occupied with railway interdiction work and the destruction of the vast petrol reserves at Châtellrault, thanks to co-operation with combined RAF Mosquito raids. Essentially, the lines Limoges–Vierzon and Poitiers–Tours were to be denied to *Das Reich*.

Captain John Tonkin   **Lieutenant Richard Crisp**   **Trooper John Fielding**

At Hassels Hall (now Hazel Hall), close to Tempsford secret airfield, on the evening of 5 June 1944, both SAS officers wiled away their time with jig-saw puzzles as they waited for their departure order. They were joined in this activity by two beautiful SOE agents, one of them being Violette Szabo, who would be taking off on her second and final mission.

Their reconniassance of the Châtellrault petrol trains was conducted by borrowed bicycle, Stephens in a borrowed civilian suit. Maquis training, parachutages, mine laying, patrols using their jeeps armed with Vickers machine guns, were interspersed with periods of enforced inactivity and near chaotic co-operation with the local Maquis, particularly on the dropping zones where French loquaciousness and politeness (*Mais, non,*

10 June 1944, Tonkin (left) and Crisp (right) flank Lieutenant Stephens who is dressed in a borrowed suit and about to set out on a reconnaissance of railway rolling stock looking for fuel transporters.

mon Capitaine! Permettez-moi! Permettez-moi!) was added to the din of bullock carts and the excited shouts of their drivers.

By the time of their arrival, Southgate's STATIONER Circuit had been broken up and the area divided between René Mainguard's SHIPWRIGHT and Pearl Witherington's WRESTLER. Jedburgh HUGH, under Captain Crawshay, came in at the same time. Received by Mainguard, who united the Jeds with the SAS, he conducted them to Neuillay-les-Bois where they made contact with Colonel Mirguet, the determined leader of the Indre FFI forces. The final SAS party arrived by 18 June and, together with the Maquis, numbered some one hundred in all. Communication with England was established by carrier pigeons, which flew at a reported speed of 100 kilometres an hour with a favourable wind and took some two to three hours to reach London.

HUGH was the first Jed team dropped into France. It had

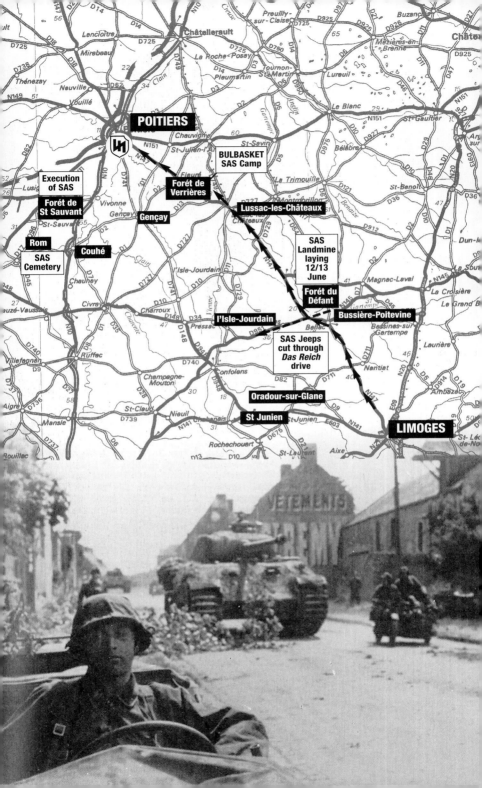

POITIERS

Execution of SAS
Forêt de St Sauvant

Rom
SAS Cemetery

Couhé

Gençay

Chauvigny

St-Julien-l'

BULBASKET SAS Camp

Forêt de Verrières

Lussac-les-Châteaux

SAS Landmine laying 12/13 June

Forêt du Défant

l'Isle-Jourdain

Bussière-Poitevine

SAS Jeeps cut through Das Reich drive

Oradour-sur-Glane

St Junien

LIMOGES

been very well briefed even to the extent of seeing photographs of the agent who was to receive them and details of the local police and Gestapo. Extremely well supplied, each officer carried 100,000 FF and the Wireless Operator, 50,000 FF. It operated for three and a half months and, between 6 June and 6 July, achieved no less than 500 rail cuts. Pearl Witherington's WRESTLER Circuit combined with René Mainguard's SHIPWRIGHT accounted for no fewer than 800 rail cuts, Pearl Witherington (MARIE) having taken over, and run, a Maquis of 2,000 men in Berry.

Battle Route

To concentrate on BULBASKET's anti-*Das Reich* activity we move to 12/13 June when Lieutenant Crisp laid mines on the N147 in the Forêt de Défant, well aware of the imminent arrival of more *Das Reich* units. Just before the forest, stop at the crossing between L'Isle-Jourdain and Bussière-Poitevine. It was here that BULBASKET's jeeps cut through *Das Reich* column, an example of 'Who Dares Wins' (D107). By 1 July they had relocated at Verrières but the Germans were already closing in, German aircraft even dropping surrender leaflets in the area. Finally, units of the SD, 17th SS Panzergrenadier Division and others moved out of Poitiers and, at dawn on Monday 3 July, launched their attack on the still sleeping SAS and Maquis.

Ruined house on the N147, Forest of Défant.
Crossroads (N147 and D107) where the SAS cut through *Das Reich* column at night.

Drive up the N147 and take the D13. To the west of the village of Verrières before entering the forest, let us leave our car and walk the Bulbasket battle route.

In this walk we were guided by the sole surviving AMILCAR Maquisard, Denis Chansigaud (HENRI), whose vivid reconstruction of the battle will enable the visitor to relive BULBASKET. Park beside the fine La Courade memorial near where T W M Stephens and seven Frenchmen met their death. Down the track to

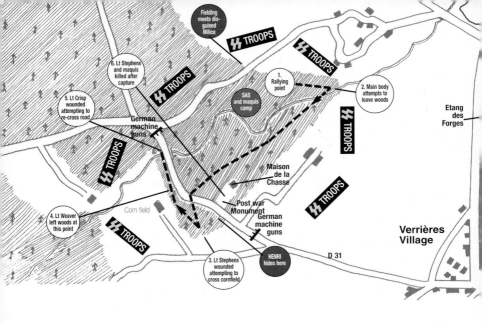

your right, towards the *Maison de la Chasse* where a German HQ had been set up, you will come across a stone marker. This is where the eight prisoners were killed. Look at the two trees behind the stone: they still bear the trace of gun shots. Return to the road and across the road to your left the narrow band of trees, at the time dense with undergrowth, is where Dennis Chansigaud hid beneath the bracken after spraying the advancing enemy with machine-gun fire and escaping through the woods to your right.

It was here he saw Stephens, after surrendering, being bludgeoned to the ground. Gunfire was erupting all around as hundreds of enemy troops swarmed through the trees. One SS soldier stood within a foot or so of him, his eyes searching, searching. He lay hidden for several hours, not moving a muscle. During this time the Germans ate their lunch, casting the shells of their hard boiled eggs into the undergrowth which hid him. Minutes later a squirrel arrived and started eating beside him. He heard the Germans cocking their guns to shoot the squirrel and he knew that if they succeeded they would discover him when they came to retrieve its body. He readied his two grenades, on the principle of 'taking some with you'. They fired, and missed the squirrel. He never sees a squirrel on his walks but that miraculous escape comes back to him. Later, a German search party came out to comb the area and he remained hidden for another one to two hours. An SS Standartenführer (Colonel) arrived and, after much *'Heil Hitler'*-ing, ordered the torture and execution of six or seven Maquisards on the road. Should he shoot the Colonel? But there were still too many Germans within a yard or two of him. When silence fell he still did not move, knowing that the Germans usually 'left' leaving one or two final look-outs hidden on the site.

Eventually he began making his escape in the direction of Verrières. As he edged forward a sudden movement ahead of him brought his heart into his mouth: he had disturbed a hare! He knew to avoid the village and moved cautiously to the lake (Etang des Forges). Here he discovered a woman with two children half submerged in the water, like him evading the Germans. Working his way around the lake he stayed there until nightfall and then set out for the nearest farm. An apprehensive response was only satisfied when he was able to identify a mutual relation by name, although it was well known that such clues were also extracted under torture by the Germans. Buried deep in hay, HENRI only requested water to ease his parched throat. The following morning he returned to the agreed RV to liaise with the other survivors.

Now, return to your car and drive down to the cross-roads ahead. This area was also packed with SS, the whole area being surrounded by some hundreds of Germans and Milice. As you cross the stream, remember that at that time the trees were old and tall and the farm to

Dennis Chansigaud, of AMILCAR, at the Verrières memorial near where he fought and lay hidden in June 1944.

The bend in the road at Verrières where John Fielding met up with the suspected informers.

Overhanging rock face in the forest where men of the SAS unit slept.

the left, also invested by SS, could not be seen. Turn right at the cross roads and drive on. At the time this was merely a farm track. Park at the edge of the woods. This was the site of John Fielding's meeting with the two Frenchmen, ostensibly from another Maquis, who turned out to be informers, probably Milice in civilian clothes. Convinced they were genuine he took them into the camp. Fielding later regretted he had not shot them on the spot.

From here walk into the forest on your right. You are soon in the centre of the camp, now marked by a small cross on a tree. The ground is undulating and, on your right, a rocky outcrop overlooks the valley. It was here the fighting began, the Germans advancing from the north. Knowing every dip and cranny the SAS and Maquis were able to eliminate many of the enemy but were forced by overwhelming numbers to retreat. HENRI described Captain Tonkin's cool direction of the battle and the stunning rapidity of the attack and defence. Camouflaged and steel-helmeted SS were blasting their way through the trees while machine-gun fire from the encircling units kept the SAS trapped. Finally, thirty-one men belonging to Operation BULBASKET were captured and, their hands manacled, were taken away.

Memorial on tree at the site of the SAS camp.

Capture and Execution

We now leave Verrières and follow these SAS men to their place of execution in the Forest of St Sauvant. Take the D13 west to Gençay (noting monuments along the route) and the D2 to Couhé. At Couhé turn north on the D7 and left at Montmatin onto the D29 for the forest itself. Left again at the sign *Stele des Fusillées* and down a forest track to the monument. The granite for the monument is said to have come from England. Here we were guided by M Gerard Daguet, who was ten years old at the time, and heard gunshots while working on his parents' farm at La Chevraise. Walk behind the monument up the original forest path and you will come across three stone markers commemorating the actual grave sites dug hastily by the Germans after their *crime de guerre*. We asked why the SAS had been brought so far from Verrières? 'They wanted to hide their crimes' M Daguet answered. (We had heard the same thing said of Oradour: the Germans had imposed a total news ban even forbidding the Bishop of Limoges to say a Mass for the victims).

SAS Monument in the Forest of St Sauvant.

Rom Communal Cemetery with the line of SAS graves.

Resistance memorials at Vaugeton.

154

Some hunters, allowed for the first time since the war began to go after sanglier (wild boar) in the forest in December 1944, noticed some cut down saplings and disturbed earth. The crime was uncovered. Exhumed and reburied in Rom Communal Cemetery the twenty-nine SAS and the American pilot Lincoln Bundy were awarded full military honours. Over at Vaugeton, (D7 northeast of the Sauvant Forest) two memorials commemorate the local dead on a site which, when discovered, was 'a sea of blood'.

For your final visit, and for the point at which we abandon *Das Reich* to the full attention of the RAF as it moved out of Resistance country and into the open beyond Poitiers, we work our way deeper into the forest.

Return to the D96 and cut across to Le Parc. Drive into the Forest by the Information Centre. If hunting and shooting is in progress stay in your car, but even then proceed with caution. On other days you can park and cover the ground on foot. Continue until you turn left up a rutted track marked La Braderie. Twisting through the trees you will come to an abandoned village.

In 1941 the ten or twelve inhabitants left it, fearing its isolation and the depradations of the enemy. Taken over by the Maquis it was used as a forest camp, their arms being hidden in the bread oven. This cache, still visible, was never discovered. Then, on 27 June 1944, as part of a punitive sweep by 2,000

Ruins of La Braderie. The well in the foreground was used by the Germans to throw bound victims.

Captured Resistance fighters about to be executed. Examples of the treatment meted out by the Germans all over France to both those who took up arms against them and innocent civilians taken hostage.

Recovery of the bodies of Resistance fighters from wells where they had been thrown to drown by the enemy. A killing technique used at Oradour-sur-Glane, La Braderie and elsewhere.

Germans and Milice, the village was searched and set on fire. Several Maquisards, trapped in the buildings, died, two being drowned, as at Oradour, in the village well.

Hidden in its silent, forest fastness La Braderie is a fitting, final point on our pilgrimage through war-time France. Birds now sing in the forest and the hunters gather to chat and reminisce. The Anglo-French memories remain. Of the SS, Wehrmacht and Milice there is no sign.

La Braderie, showing the bread oven used as an arms cache.

Circuit: FIREMAN
Dates: March – September 1944
Principal Departments: HAUTE VIENNE, CREUSE and
ALLIER

Run by the Mayer brothers, Percy and Edmund
(BARTHELEMY and MAURICE respectively) they had
parachuted in on 7 March 1944, in the Lot. They were followed,
on 22 March, by Paddy O'Sullivan (SIMONET) as wireless
operator. Paddy O'Sullivan was received by Gaston Collin who
told me that, shaken and bruised on landing with a
malfunctioning parachute, she attributed her survival to the
bundles of French banknotes wrapped around her. Paddy was,
he said, an explosive mixture of Irish and Breton blood,
attractive and high spirited. She had once thrown a chair at her
SOE instructor. Only partially trained, this twenty six year old
girl transmitted 332 messages over a seven month period in
spite of suffering from chronic bronchitis. Her understanding of
security was nil, 'constantly losing and running after bits of
paper and tearing up messages which had either been or not
been transmitted'. She could not even ride a bicycle. The luck of
the Irish saw her through and she was, in her chief's words: 'a
first class W/T and all the credit for that was entirely due to
herself'. FIREMAN was a liaison Circuit with the VENY groups
involved in arms supply, sabotage and guerilla training. They
saw effective action against *Das Reich* and, at the end, received
this citation from Colonel FRANÇOIS of the MUR: 'Let me tell
you how grateful I am for the actions you carried out . . . We owe
to you the Military Organisation of this Sector; we owe to you
the not inconsiderable results which have been achieved there. I
shall never forget what the Creuse owes to you'.

Percy Mayer was awarded the OBE and MC, his brother
Edmund the MBE. Paddy O'Sullivan received the MBE.

A bullock-drawn cart being loaded with a container, the usual method used by Resistants for retrieving arms and supplies.

Circuit: SHIPWRIGHT
Dates: May 1944 – September 1944
Principal Departments: CREUSE, ALLIER, INDRE, VIENNE and HAUTE VIENNE.

Following Southgate's arrest 1 May 1944, at Montluçon, Roger Mainguard (SAMUEL) took command of the STATIONER Circuit which he divided into three sectors. His new SHIPWRIGHT Circuit included Jacques Hirsch (ARTHUR) who established contact with SURCOUF, Chief of the *Armée Secrète* in Indre and ELLIPSE (Eugene Dechelette) the DM of Region 5. Mainguard was acknowledged by the French as an outstanding agent: a few days after D-Day he had over 5,000 men under his direct command. By August of 1944 he had 5,000 in Vienne; 3,000 in Haute Vienne; 2,000 in Deux-Sévres; and 2,000 in the Vendée ready for arms. Other agents working with SAMUEL included Lieutenant Dane, a weapons and Dakota expert; Lieutenant Wallace and two Americans, Lieutenants Blackwell and MacCarthy.

He was awarded the DSO and the *Croix de Guerre avec Palmes* by General Köenig.

Circuit: WRESTLER
Dates: May 1944 – October 1944
Principal Departments: NORTH INDRE and PUY de DÔME.

Pearl Witherington (MARIE) took over on 1 May to run the Northern Indre sector of the old STATIONER Circuit which she had worked with since September 1943. She had already made contact with ANASTASIE (Jacques Dufour) and was involved in sabotage operations in Salon-la-Tour. When the German and Vichy French troops encircled Montluçon she decided to break through the cordon which she succeeded in doing in company with Henri Charles Cornioley (her future husband). She then organised her Circuit in four sections and coordinated groups of Maquis at the Château des Souches. In a ten hour battle the Germans lost eighty-six killed and 200 wounded, the Maquis twenty-four but the attack had disorganised the Maquis and a new start had to be made. To co-operate with the French Army she had to bring in two officers, with whom she worked in complete harmony until the Liberation. MARIE organised over 23 extremely difficult and vital parachute drops. In August her 800 strong sub-sector under COMPTE was surrounded by some 4,000 to 6,000 Germans. The battle was extremely violent, the Germans losing 180 killed and 300 wounded against COMPTE's total loss of twenty-two.

Congratulated by General Eisenhower for reporting the movement of sixty German armoured trains on their way to Normandy at the time of the Allied landings, Pearl Witherington was awarded the MBE and *Croix de Guerre avec Palmes* and later presented to HM The Queen.

Pearl Witherington

The air above northern France was alive with Allied aircraft making all movement by the German forces a dangerous undertaking. Hawker Typhoon with D-Day livery.
This 75mm StuG III resembles a moving bush and any air activity would cause its crew to stop immediately.

CHAPTER ELEVEN

DAS REICH – RENDERING AN ACCOUNT

The Fighting in Normandy

The end of *Das Reich* has an element of nemesis.

Having escaped the Maquis, only to be decimated by the RAF as it moved out of Resistance country near Poitiers, it was to re-enter the war against the Allies at St-Lô on 26 June. This was eighteen days following its departure from Montauban having spent eight days in the area meticulously camouflaging their vehicles and generally lying-low. St-Lô was described by Weidinger as a 'no-man's-land' having been totally destroyed by Allied air attacks.

Then, on 16 June, *Das Reich* signalled: 'Enemy – English 11th Armoured Division has crossed the Odon... is pushing deep into the front of the 12th SS Panzer Division *Hitler-Jugend* ...' The clash of giants had begun.

It is impossible here to adequately trace their total

Saturation Allied air dominance hinders *Das Reich* movement in Normandy.

Das Reich officers and men captured at Notre Dame de Cenilly 28 July, 1944, by elements of the US 2nd Armored Division. They are believed to be from the *Deutschland* Regiment.

Das Reich panzer ace Oberscharführer Ernst Barkmann who destroyed thirteen Sherman tanks in Normandy in his Panther. He was not involved in the 'Lammerding Pacifications'. He survived the war.

involvement in the battle of Normandy nor their subsequent actions until the fall of Germany. The specialist literature is more than enough for that. In Normandy they moved from St-Lô into annihilation battles at Villers-Bocage and Noyers, south east of Caen, where Diekmann was reported killed on 30 June. Here *Das Reich* was reporting 'hurricane force' artillery fire and they were pulled back, with 40% losses, to Jurques on 2 July.

Transferred to the Cotentin Peninsular, at Le-Haye-de-Puits, then south to Mortain, by 17 August they were to enter the Falaise Pocket. Here

Smashed men and equipment caught in the Falaise Pocket. The way to Paris was open to the Allies and the Germans were streaming back through France along the 'Corridor of Death'.

the *Der Führer* was to report: 'Pocket opened near Champesoult... units streaming east out of the pocket'. The following figures must tell the story:

10,000	German soldiers		killed
40,000	"	"	taken prisoner
50,000	"	"	escaped

Amongst those who got away were two Commanding Generals and over 300 senior officers who came out on foot with the soldiers. They called it 'the Stalingrad of Normandy'. *Das Reich* escaped through the 'Corridor of Death' at Montormel.

Germany, The Ardennes, Hungary, Vienna and Prague

Of its subsequent retreats and counter-attacks through France to Germany's *WESTWALL* in early September the reader must study elsewhere. They were to enter the Ardennes Offensive on 23 December but in spite of initial successes by 17 January they were pulled out with losses running to about 35% of combat strength plus another 10% due to frostbite. They returned to Germany until early February when they moved to

The end nears for these men of *Das Reich*.

Commander of *Der Führer* Regiment Otto Weiddinger (facing camera) consults with fellow officers in Austria in 1945. Uppermost on their minds would likely be their fate if taken captive by the Russians.

Hungary to fight the Red Army; withdrawn again to defend the Reich under the so-called *Führer Order* they participated in the defence of Vienna; and retreated to Prague where they fought their last battle on 8 May 1945.

Thus from the *Der Führer* came their final words: 'Mission accomplished... surrender to the Americans... signing off. Long live Germany'.

Surrender And Captivity

Marching out of Prague on 9 May they were met by an unknown German General and a Czech Colonel. Here they were ordered to hand over their weapons. The war chests were emptied and the men paid out. At the end of the day they entered the town of Rokyczany and captivity.

Later they were transferred to the former concentration camp of Flossenburg in Germany ('everyone breathed a sigh of relief: the danger of a handover to Russia was gone!'), others to Regensburg, then to Landshut and, in Germany, finally to the Regensburg Civilian Internee Camp. By the second half of 1947 the final release of its inmates began. But, more was to come.

The Trials

Numbers of SS were collected in the former concentration camp of Dachau by a French Commission. These were later transferred to France and on 18 November 1947, arrived in Bordeaux. Two years later, in 1950, the actual interrogations began in connection with the attrocity at Oradour. The upshot of the several trials that were held may be summarised: 1951 and 1953, two death sentences commuted, all other sentences amnestied except that of the Alsatian Unterscharführer (Sergeant) Boos. In East Berlin in 1983 Obersturmführer (Lieutenant) Barth was sentenced to life imprisonment. For the Tulle hangings, only three accused were available: all found guilty, they were set free after a few months in 1952. Lammerding, sentenced to death *in absentia*, died in his bed in 1971.

We can now follow the main *Das Reich* protagonists into oblivion.

General Lammerding, as already noted, died in retirement on 14 January 1971, in his Bavarian home at Greiling and was buried, 19 January, in the North Cemetery at Düsseldorf. Two

GREN.
GEORG BÖSSL
*9.12.20 +9.6.44

STUBAF.
ADOLF DIEKMANN
*18.19.14 +29.6.44

Adolf Diekmann is buried at Marigny, France. He was killed in action 29 June 1944.

hundred ex-SS, including Colonel Weidinger, attended the funeral. Major Stückler became a main-stay of the *Waffen SS* Old Comrades Association and its bulletin, *Der Freiwillige*.

On 17 April 1959, the last returnee from France was, after fourteen years of captivity, given a new start in life with a three week holiday in the Tyrol with a former comrade. Colonel Weidinger became a prolific historian of the *Waffen SS* and died in January 1990. His widow graciously gave me her authority to quote from his book *Comrades to the End*, (a book, incidentally, banned in France). Kämpfe and Diekmann we have traced as far as possible. Kahn 'disappeared' in the Normandy inferno. Barth was condemned to life imprisonment in East Berlin in 1983. For Barth, Oradour was a totally normal activity and he could make no sense of the accusations: he had previously participated in the massacre of 476 victims at Lidice in Czechoslovakia on 10 June 1943. His main regret in prison was that he was deprived of seeing his grandchildren.

Bordeaux 1947

Of the post-war trials special mention must be made of those at Bordeaux in 1947, 1951 and 1953; at Natzweiler in 1945; and at Wuppertal in 1947.

In 1947, sixty men of *Das Reich* were collected from Dachau by a French Commission under Captain Tretnel. By 18 November the former Commander of the *Der Führer* was also delivered to the military jail in Bordeaux. After accusing him of the Tulle atrocity, the court waited for a year, the investigating judge, Captain Lesieur, 'uncertain as to how to go about investigating such a complex case'. Then, in 1948, it was announced that many of the accused could go home with a *non lieu* (dropping of the case) but nothing happened.

Later the *Lex Oradour* was passed. This meant that anyone could be considered as a perpetrator even if he was only a member at the same time in the same area as a unit accused of war crimes. Additionally, the burden of proof was passed to the accused. A strip of land approximately thirty kilometers wide of the march route was designated the trial area. Two years later, in 1950, the actual interrogations began, batches of the accused

Accused Alsatians who were directly involved in the attrocity at Oradour-sur-Glane, along with eight other ex-members of the *Der Führer* Regiment, on trial at Bordeaux in 1953.

being delivered to Bordeaux from the prison in Périgeux. In the spring of 1951 the majority of the cases were dropped and the 1951 trial concentrated on fifty accused. The verdict: *'Tous acquittés!'*.

The next day the ex SS men travelled back via Paris, where they went sight-seeing, to Tuttlingen where they received their French release papers. A few more trials followed in Bordeaux: all but a handful were found 'Not guilty' and were returned to Germany. By 1959, everyone was home. In German eyes this was a complete vindication of their innocence, an innocence confirmed by a French court. In 1953, the thirteen Alsatian members of *Das Reich*, involved directly with Oradour, went on trial along with the eight remaining German SS. On the evening before the verdict all the Alsatians were amnestised by the French Government in the name of national reunification. Five of the Germans were immediately repatriated; two were condemned to hard labour; one was proven to be mentally ill and was transferred to hospital.

Indignation exploded throughout France: a protest march in Limoges counted 50,000 people. In Oradour, the *Croix de Guerre* and the *Légion d'Honneur* were removed from the Town Hall and the cemetery respectively and returned to the Government in

169

Entrance to Natzweiler-Struthof Concentration Camp in Alsace. Built by the Germans, after the war it was used to house those suspected of war crimes.

Paris. Two boards, one listing the Alsatians and the part they were reported to have taken in the massacre, the other a list of the 319 Parliamentary Deputies, along with their supporting Senators, who had voted the amnesty, were put on display at the entrance to the ruins and remained there until 1966.

New Oradour, a town of some 2,000 people, has sprung up alongside the ruins of the old. A visit to the Church of St Martin is recommended. Here you will see one of the rare, surviving statues from the old church. Also in Oradour, a great *Centre de la Mémoire* has been built to help clarify the events at Oradour for the many who visit there each summer.

For lunch: Restaurant La Glane in the Place Général de Gaulle.

Natzweiler, 1945

The Natzweiler Trial of 1945 was the upshot of Vera Atkins' single-minded hunt for the missing F Section SOE agents after the war. She had combined forces with Captain Yurka Galazine, a young British officer of White Russian and English descent, and Major Bill Barkworth, SAS's Intelligence Officer. They worked under the aegis of the Political Warfare Department of SHAEF and their hunt started at Natzweiler camp. Amongst the records there they came across some drawings signed, B J Stonehouse. Temporarily commissioned into the WAAF and attached to the War Crimes Investigation Unit in the British Zone, Vera Atkins moved from Natzweiler back to England where she made contact with Odette Sanson, recently returned from Ravensbrück, and Brian Stonehouse, recently returned from Dachau. Stonehouse was a witness to the execution of four women F Section agents at Natzweiler. Meanwhile, Barkworth was on the trail of missing SAS troops, executed by the Germans in the Vosges. Following up the trail in Germany, Vera Atkins was able to interrogate several SS responsible for the three camps. Finally, at the trial, the grim evidence came out and law, if not justice, was observed.

Wuppertal, 1947

For the SAS, the priority was to discover the fate of the men of the BULBASKET Mission. Again, a long haul led Barkworth to giving evidence in March 1947 against Generals Blumentritt and Gallenkamp, Colonel Koestlin, Captain Schönig, Lieutenant Deter and Doctors Tönshoff, Hesterberg and Weber in the case of the unlawful killing of thirty-one SAS in and near the Forest of Verrières, 3 July 1944. Four were acquitted but Gallenkamp and Hersterberg were sentenced to death by hanging. Following appeal, Gallenkamp was finally released in 1952 and Hesterberg was set free. The fate of Koestlin is unclear from the files.

Thirty-one SAS of BULBASKET are buried in Rom Communal Cemetery near the Forest of Saint-Sauvat where they were executed. Lieutenant T W N Stephens' tomb is in the vault of the Mangier and de Montjon family in the cemetery at Gençay. Fine memorials have been erected at La Courade in the Verrières Forest and at Saint-Sauvat. In September 1998, seven ex-SAS, under Major Schofield, returned to pay homage, accompanied by a large group of ex-Maquis. Once again the Tricolour and the Union Jack flew together under an autumn sky.

The French

Any list of French heroes and heroines of the Resistance in the ten SOE Circuit areas must be incomplete and invidious. I have therefore confined my selection to those names included in the Circuit chiefs' reports and Maurice Buckmaster's fact finding JUDEX Mission.

In the PIMENTO area, first reference must go to Tony Brooks' crucial contact, CHARLES (later ROBERT) the SNCF Trade Unionist who put ALPHONSE in touch with the *cheminots*. Pierre and Madame, Bloch; Max Hymans (later Minister of Civil Aviation); Gaston Gusin, Vichy administrator but actually an SIS agent; and Michel Comte, Garage des Pyrénées, Montauban.

In WHEELWRIGHT, Roger Larribeau, Mayor of Castelnau-sous-L'Avignon; BERGERET, actually Maurice Loupias, Sub-Prefect of Bergerac; Maurice Parisot, Commandant Battalion d'Armagnac; Aldo Molesini, wood merchant; Antoine Merchez, garage owner; J Novarini, Italian peasant; B Alessandri, saboteur.

In FOOTMAN, Henri Collignon, *Groups Vény*; Jean-Jacques Chapou (FTP, Lot and Corrèze); Commandant Cavallier, *Groups Vény* (Tarn); the Verhlac family, cheese manufacturers; Captain and Madame Jean Veilliac; Georges Bru; and Pierre and Odette Bach of the 'stray dogs home' in Figeac.

In STATIONER, the Néraud family, the father dying in Buchenwald, the mother in Ravensbrück, only the daughter, Collette, returning; Jacques Hirsch, safe house and couriers; Georges Audouard of the Terrasson Maquis; M Delord, Maquis organiser; Raymond Reinier, safe house, wireless transmission, parachutages.

In his book Jacques Poirier lists no fewer than fifty specially mentioned Resistants in AUTHOR/DIGGER. Here we may mention: Maurice Arnouilh; Madelaine Bleygeat; Charles Brouilhet, THE BOLSHEVIK, and his wife, Marguerite; André Gaucher (MARTIAL); Marius Guédin, *Armée Secrète*, Corrèze; Paul and Georgette Lachaud; Abbé Marchadoux, parish priest of Sarlat; Colonel Robert Poirier; and René Vaujour, *Armée Secrète*, Corrèze.

French Resistants pay homage to SOE at the SOE F Section Monument at Valençay, 6 May 1997.

In VENTRILOQUIST mention must be made of Octave Chantraine, President of the *Fédération Paysanne de l'Indre*, crucial in the parachutages around Châteauroux; Charles Rechmann, ex-Army officer; and Stanislav Makowski, captured and tortured to death near Romarantin, 23 August 1944. He is buried in Pornic War Cemetery, Loire-Atlantique, Grave ref 2 AB 17.

SALESMAN 2: Georges Guingouin, FFI Chief, Haute Vienne, elected Mayor of Limoges, 1945; Commandant Huard, *Armée Secrète*; Captain Rolet, FFI Company *Le Desert*, battle of Châteauneuf.

FIREMAN: Lieutenant Col Francois, *Mouvements Unifiés de la Résistance*; Commandant Maldart, MUR; Commandant Melon, FTP.

SHIPWRIGHT: Eugene Deschelette (ELLIPSE); SURCOUF of the *Armée Secrète* in Indre; M Villeuneuve at Montmorillon.

WRESTLER: M & Mme Sabassier; M & Mme Trochet; Commandant Francis Perdiset and Captain Pierre Mercier; and Captains Emile Gouman, Camille Boiziau, Perrot and Vannier.

To put this limited selection of names into some perspective we should recognize that 'best estimates' reckon the Resistance numbered around some 125,000/150,000 'effectives' out of a total of some 450,000 throughout France.

Kaltenbrunner, the Nazi chief of Police services in France, in his report of June 1943, estimated 80,000 effectives in the *Armée Secrète* alone.

According to Henry Michel, in his *Histoire de la Résistance* of 1950, more than 30,000 Resistants were shot and many more were deported.

Women (and even children in a number of cases) made a very significant contribution to the Resistance and this was acknowledged by the Government when French women were awarded the right to vote after the war for their heroism. As Francis Cammaerts told me, 'without the women we could have done nothing'.

The British

Of the British agents' subsequent lives I can only write of the little I know from personal contacts.

Following the order of March, PIMENTO's Tony Brooks has always been closely involved with all post-war SOE affairs and is a wide ranging source on SOE matters. Sadly, I just missed meeting WHEELWRIGHT's wonder wireless operator, Yvonne Cormeau, who died while this book was in the writing. FOOTMAN's George Hiller became a brilliant diplomat and died in Belgium in 1962. His widow, Judith Hiller, has not only been a charming hostess in her home in the Lot but has provided innumerable introductions and insights. Cyril Watney lives in England, Gaston Collins in Paris: both assisted me.

Jacques Poirier's career in the oil industry took him over half the world. Without his tireless attention to my questions, and the aid of his book, I would have committed many more errors than I might have done. Peter Lake also became a diplomat, in two continents, and his contribution is gratefully acknowledged. Ralph Beauclerc became a successful banker and through mutual friends, the Greigs, provided me with detailed information on his wireless days.

Geoffrey Staunton is commemorated in Limoges, having a street named after him. Violette Szabo, the first British woman to be awarded the George Cross, has a blue commemorative plaque on her home at No 18 Burnley Road, Brixton and her name is included on the FANY memorial at St Paul's, Knightsbridge. Her year 2000 commemoration in Sussac has been noted.

Brian Stonehouse, whom I met at the Valençay reunion in 1997, died in December 1998 after a distinguished art career. Francis Cammaerts, who lives in France, and Roger Landes, who lives in England, have both been generous with their time and knowledge. Pearl Cornioley is still active in SOE circles and Vera Atkins was, right up to her death 16 June 2000, an outspoken spokeswoman for the agents and their families. She gave me freely of her time both in London and at her country home. I am honoured that she gave me permission to dedicate this book to her.

Daphne Friele, of the Jeds, gave me unlimited access to her Milton Hall archives and our visits to her home in Brittany were always a joy. She now lives in the USA. John Fielding has provided invaluable insights into BULBASKET and Hugh Verity politely corrected my erroneous ideas on how a Lysander landed.

The Spirit of Resistance lives on.

CHAPTER TWELVE

EYEWITNESS

This is the testimony of a French youth who survived those dangerous years, and the passing through the heart of France of the 2nd SS Panzer Division Das Reich.

Monsieur S was twenty years of age when he joined the Maquis. In fact, he became the member of two groups of Resistants, the FTP and the *Armée Secrète*. On their amalgamation with the ORA they formed the 4th Regiment, under the command of Lieutenant-Colonel Guingouin. Monsieur S was directly involved in actions against *Das Reich*. Herewith his testimony.

In his village, everyone was Communist, you were obliged to be so. This did not mean that some were not also Christians: one thing was political, the other was religion. His mother wanted him to become a priest and he now rather regrets that he did not. At the time it was not so clear and his father objected. Indeed, the girls would not kiss him when it became known!

His father died when he was eleven years old and he lived and worked on a farm. He was rather nervous when he went into the Resistance but he could get home from time to time. As the Maquis became armed, their confidence grew. Parachute drops in the area became more frequent and he vividly recalls his first experience. It was at night and very cold. They built small signal fires at different angles and commanded the drop with the aid of an electric lamp. Then, they heard the plane come over. It circled and went away. He thought the drop had been abandoned but was told the pilot was checking the signal code and would return. Then, they heard its engines again and down floated the containers. They had to bury the parachutes quickly and struggle with the containers. The English had thought of everything: arms, ammunition, chocolate, tobacco, clothing, even a camera. He was horrified to find huge quantities of bandages and this rather diminished his enthusiasm for the fighting to come. Then they had to try and eliminate the signs of the fires. The next morning, local people came out and found the embers. They decided that it was *sorcellerie*, the work of local witches!

Another parachutage involved money, huge quantities of French francs, some of them real, some of them false, they thought. They took some to the Post Office but they wanted to know where the money came from. They hid the money in tombs in the cemetery.

As soon as the young men were armed, they thought they could do anything. The Maquis chief was Georges Guingouin. He was strong and exerted a firm command. He was tough and did some terrible things but without him the situation would have been far worse. There was a lot of indiscipline and other Maquis bands came in, even from as far away as Clermont-Ferrand, and stole everything. Guingouin set a price on food supplies against the black market prices: a maximum of 80F for a kilo of butter, or 4F for a kilo of potatoes. Monsieur S was appalled by the banditry and jealousy. Someone would say that they knew where there was a lot of good wine. Then they would go out and steal it. Jealousy, he said, was the main cause of crimes such as this. Against this, Guingouin would set his regulations but they were not always observed. He was quite merciless when people were found out. He did however manage to maintain order and you always knew where you stood with him. (This is in exact agreement with Major Staunton's SOE report).

Once armed, the Maquis wanted to attack the enemy but it was not that simple. The Milice was also very active and, in many ways, worse than the Germans. He was deeply shocked to see what Frenchmen would do to Frenchmen: a couple blindfolded, tied to a tree, and then shot. You never knew why.

Two incidents stood out in his memory. First, the famous parachutage of 26 June 1944, when seventy-two Flying Fortresses, supported by RAF fighters, launched 864 containers: he can never forget the overwhelming experience of that day. Second, the arrival, in uniform, of a British officer (he cannot recall his name) who was extremely tall and commanding. He was armed with a sub-machine gun in one hand and a grenade in the other as he landed. S hoped the grenade would not go off! He showed them how to react to the presence of enemy forces and S found this equally frightening! They were not used to obeying orders in such a way. He is not sure what happened to the British officer. He was not very popular and he last saw him in a wood. (Other Resistants have told me that sometimes agents parachuted in were killed by the Maquis which did not want any outside influence. I am not saying this was the case here. S was very low down in the Maquis hierarchy and he makes no claim to knowledge outside his personal experience).

Attacks by the Maquis on German columns in the area were very dangerous. He was witness to one such: the Maquis opened fire from the edge of the road. Immediately, the Germans sprang from their vehicles and, in no time at all, had encircled the Maquis and annihilated them. They were professionals, the Maquis were shot down like rabbits.

Following the night of 5 June 1944, (*Plan Vert* was announced in Haute-Vienne by the BBC with the message, 'In the forest there is a great tree') they were alerted to the arrival of *Das Reich*. He described his witness of this unit.

The noise of their arrival was terrific. He could see the soldiers, all perfectly disciplined, young and dressed for combat. Guingouin ordered that they should not mine the roads as they were completely surrounded by SS troops and such a move would have been fatal. Furthermore, he explained that with their armoured, caterpillar tracks they could easily swing past any exploded area in the road.

He saw how *Das Reich* prepared for action against the 'terrorists'. They set up machine guns and, using explosive bullets, cut down the trees, even oaks as big as six inches across, at the height of a man to give themselves a field of fire. He was in hiding. Then, making his way across a remote area, carrying his revolver, he was astonished to find that enemy units were coming down a muddy farm track, miles from anywhere. They were, in fact, everywhere, combing the countryside for 'terrorists'. They scanned the countryside with binoculars and were in communication by radio. Milice informers would identify camps and Maquis units. He threw himself to the ground, hid in a ditch and said his prayers: he had no desire to be awarded a posthumous decoration! He was, he said, not very brave, not a real maquisard.

Even after the passage of *Das Reich* they would send units back to pacify the region. There were many unfortunate events. Erroneously, in his opinion, some Resistants thought that the parish priest had disclosed the whereabouts of two camps. They thought he had a wireless transmitter in his presbytery but in fact it was an ordinary radio, only capable of receiving regular transmissions. The priest used it to listen to the BBC. In the event, he was assassinated.

S is now eighty years old and one of the few remaining Resistants in his area. There are others, but mostly rather unwilling to talk. In the woods around are buried the last big supplies of arms, some of which they buried beside the lakes to avoid discovery since, at the end, they had more than enough. It was his job, with two others, to guard a huge dump of arms and plastic explosive, tons of it. But, he said, what could they do if the Germans arrived?

From here, we set out into the woods to rediscover the arms hidden there for over fifty years. For the visitor today, there is much to discover along the line of march of *Das Reich*.

The Author with a German Gewehr 98 which has been dug up at the Maquis camp at Aigueperse, where it had lain hidden for fifty-six years along with Sten guns and other weaponry.

'We feel sure that nothing of which we have any knowledge or record has ever been done by mortal men which surpasses the splendour and daring of their feats of arms.'
WINSTON S CHURCHILL, WESTMINSTER ABBEY, 21 MAY 1948, ON THE WORK OF THE SPECIAL FORCES.

Bibliography

NOTE ON PRINCIPAL SOURCES

GENERAL

ENGLISH

SOE IN FRANCE – An Account of the Work of the British Special
Operations Executive in France, 1940–1944, M R D Foot, HMSO 1966
(The indispensable authorised history)
THEY FOUGHT ALONE – The Story of British Agents in France,
Maurice Buckmaster, Odhams, London, 1958
F SECTION SOE – The Buckmaster Networks, Marcel Ruby, Leo
Cooper, London, 1985
INSIDE SOE – The Story of Special Operations in Western Europe
1940–1945, E H Cookridge, Arthur Barker, London, 1966
SECRET WAR – The Story of SOE, Britain's Wartime Sabotage
Organisation, Nigel West, Hodder & Stoughton, London, 1992
MISSION IMPROBABLE – A Salute to the RAF Women of SOE in
France, Beryl Escott, Patrick Stevens, Sparkford, 1991
SABOTAGE & SUBVERSION – Stories from the Files of the SOE and
OSS, Ian Dear, Arms & Armour, London, 1996
UNDERCOVER – Men and Women of the SOE, Patrick Howarth,
Routledge & Kegan Paul, London 1980

ARCHIVES

FOREIGN & COMMONWEALTH OFFICE, SOE Advisor, Whitehall,
London
PUBLIC RECORD OFFICE, Kew, Surrey
IMPERIAL WAR MUSEUM, Lambeth Road, London
MILTON HALL JEDBURGH ARCHIVES
BBC INFORMATION & ARCHIVES, Broadcasting House, London
NATIONAL ARCHIVES AT COLLEGE PARK, Maryland, USA
CENTRAL INTELLIGENCE AGENCY, Langley, Virginia, USA
FÉDÉRATION NATIONALE FFC LIBRE RÉSISTANCE, Paris
MUSÉE DE L'ORDRE DE LA LIBÉRATION, Paris (Metro: Latour
Mauberg)
BRITISH CONSULATE-GENERAL, Bordeaux
COMMONWEALTH WAR GRAVES COMMISSION, Beaurains

FRENCH
HISTOIRE DE LA RÉSISTANCE, F-G Dreyfus, Fallois, Paris, 1996
      (Above sources apply generally throughout the Guide)

CHAPTER 1

ENGLISH

DAS REICH – The March of the 2nd Panzer Division through France June 1944, Max Hastings, Michael Joseph, London, 1981
MOONDROP TO GASCONY, Anne-Marie Walters, Macmillan, London, 1946
PIMENTO: SOE Archives R1, R2, R3, R4, Sheet 28
WHEELWRIGHT: SOE Archives R4, Sheet 42

FRENCH

R5 – LES SS EN LIMOUSIN & QUERCY, Beau & Gaubussian, Presses de la Cité, Paris, 1984
DAS REICH ET LA COEUR DE LA FRANCE, Guicheteau, Daniel, Paris, 1974
LA RÉSISTANCE DANS LA SUD-OUEST, Dominique Lormier, Sud-Ouest, 1989
LA RÉSISTANCE EN TARN-ET-GARONNE, ANACR, Montauban, 1989
LES RÉSEAUX ET ACTION DE LA FRANCE COMBATTANTS 1940–1944, Amicale des Réseaux Action de la France
GUERRES MONDIALES & CONFLICTS CONTEMPORAINES, 152 & 164, David Wingate-Price
MUSÉE DE LA RÉSISTANCE DE LA DÉPORTATION DE LA LIBÉRATION du Département du Lot, Bessières, Cahors. Tel: 05 65 22 14 25
MUSÉE DE LA RÉSISTANCE ET DE LA DÉPORTATION en Tarn-et-Garonne, Montauban. Tel: 05 63 66 03 11

GERMAN

COMRADES TO THE END - The 4th SS Panzer-Grenadier Regiment *Der Führer* 1938–1945, Otto Weidinger, Schiffer, PA, USA

CHAPTER 2

ENGLISH

TEMPSFORD AIRFIELD, Bernard O'Connor, Maythyme, 1991
CARPETBAGGERS, L R Dick, Flight Journal, Feb 1999
WE LANDED BY MOONLIGHT, Hugh Verity, Ian Allan, London 1979
MISSION BY MOONLIGHT, British SOE and American OSS Special Operations in Central South West France, Philip Vickers, unpublished msc, 1998

FRENCH

HISTOIRE DE LA RÉSISTANCE EN FRANCE, Jean-François, Presses Universitaire de France
MUSÉE CHARENTAIS DE LA RÉSISTANCE ET DE LA DÉPORTATION, Angoulême. Tel: 05 45 38 76 87

CHAPTER 3

ENGLISH
THE STRUGGLE FOR EUROPE, Chester Wilmot, Collins, London, 1952
STRUGGLE FOR SURVIVAL – The History of the Second World War, R
A C Parker, Oxford, 1989
SOLDIERS OF THE NIGHT – The Story of the French Resistance, David
Schoenbrun, New American Library,New York, 1989
MOST SECRET WAR – British Scientific Intelligence 1939–1945, R V
Jones, Hodder & Stoughton, 1978
SPECIAL DUTY OPERATIONS, R McLeod, ATB
ULTRA, R Bennet, ATB
D-DAY MUSEUM, Portsmouth, Hampshire

FRENCH
MUSÉE POUR LA PAIX & POUR COMPRENDRE LE XXe SIÈCLE,
Caen, Normandy. Tel: 02 31 06 06 44

GERMAN
D-DAY – An Appreciation, G von Rundstedt, ATB
DIE INVASION HAT BEGONNEN!, B Zimmermann, ATB
GERMAN DEFENCES, B Zimmermann, ATB

CHAPTER 4

FRENCH
LA RÉSISTANCE DANS LE SUD-OUEST, Dominique Lormier, Sud-
Ouest, 1989
LES RÉSEAUX ET ACTION DE LA FRANCE COMBATTANTS
1940–1944, Amicale des Réseaux Action de la France
OMBRES ET ESPÉRANCES EN QUERCY – Armé Secrète et Groupes
Vény du Lot 1940–1945, Bru, Picard & Chaussade, Privat, Toulouse, 1980

CHAPTER 5

ENGLISH
THE GIRAFFE HAS A LONG NECK, Jacques Poirier, Leo Cooper,
London, 1995
AUTHOR/DIGGER: SOE ARCHIVES R5, R4, Sheets 39/40
FOOTMAN: SOE ARCHIVES R4, Sheet 26

FRENCH
ANDRÉ MALRAUX ET LA RÉSISTANCE, G Penaud, Fanlac, Périgueux,
1986
HISTOIRE DE LA RÉSISTANCE EN PÉRIGORD, G Penaud, Fanlac,
Périgueux, 1991
LA RÉSISTANCE EN DORDOGNE 1939–40 à 1945 – La Lutte contre le
nazisme et le régime de Vichy, ANACR, Moderne, 1996

MAQUIS DE CORRÈZE, Collectif Maquis de la Corrèze, Musée Tulle, 1995
MUSÉE DE LA RÉSISTANCE ET DE LA DÉPORTATION, Tulle. Tel: 05 55 26 24 36
1944 EN DORDOGNE, J Lagrange, Pilote, Périgueux, 1993
COMPTE RENDU DES ACTIVITÉS D'UN RADIO ANGLAIS PARACHUTÉ EN FRANCE PENDANT L'OCCUPATION, R Beauclerc, msc 1989
ROUTE DE LA LIBERTÉ, M M Fourcade, CN RD, Brive
CENTRE NATIONAL DE LA RÉSISTANCE ET DE LA DÉPORTATION, Musée Edmond Michelet, Brive Tel: 05 55 74 06 08

CHAPTER 6
ENGLISH
CARVE HER NAME WITH PRIDE, R J Minney, Newnes, London, 1956; J Arthur Rank film; T Popple, ATB
SALESMAN 2: SOE ARCHIVES A2, R5, Sheet 22
VENTRILOQUIST: SOE ARCHIVES B1, R5 P2, Sheet 9
VIOLETTE SZABO MILLENNIUM MUSEUM, Hereford, Tel: 01981-540477

FRENCH
LES ARTISANS DE LA LIBERTÉ, Philippe de Vomécourt, Pac, Paris, 1961 (WHO LIVED TO SEE THE DAY, Hutchinson, London)
QUATRE ANS SUR LE SOL LIMOUSIN, Georges Guinguoin, Hachette, Paris, 1978
L'OMBRE DE MARÉCHAL, de Cedouy & Follin, France 2 TV, 1995

CHAPTER 7
FRENCH
21 AOÛT 44 LIMOGES LIBÉRÉE, A Rodet, 1994
MUSÉE DE LA RÉSISTANCE DU DÉPARTEMENT DE LA HAUTE-VIENNE, Limoges Tel: 05 55 45 63 85

CHAPTER 8
FRENCH
ORADOUR – PLUS PRÈS DE LA VÉRITÉ, P Maysounave, Souny, 1996
LA RÉGION DE ST-PAUL-D'EYJEAUX EN LIMOUSIN DURANT LA SECONDE GUERRE MONDIALE, Yves Soulignac, La Veytizou, 1993
LA MILICE – La Collaboration en Uniforme, Historia No 40, 1975

CHAPTER 9
ENGLISH
ORADOUR: VILLAGE OF THE DEAD, P Beck, Leo Cooper, London, 1979

FRENCH
ORADOUR: LE DRAME HEURE PAR HEURE, R Hébras, CMD,
Montreuil-Bellay, 1992
CENTRE DE LA MÉMOIRE, Oradour-sur-Glane.
Tel: 05 55 43 04 30

CHAPTER 10
ENGLISH
OPERATION BULBASKET – Behind the Lines in Occupied France 1944,
P McCue, Pen & Sword, Leo Cooper, London, 1996
THE SAS, THE OFFICIAL HISTORY, P Warner, Warner Books, 1993
NOW IT CAN BE TOLD, Trustees of the IWM, DD Video
STATIONER: SOE ARCHIVES R4, R5, Sheet 30
FIREMAN: SOE ARCHIVES R5, B2, Sheet 26
SHIPWRIGHT: SOE ARCHIVES B2, R5, Sheet 30A
WRESTLER: SOE ARCHIVES R5, Sheet 27

CHAPTER 11
ENGLISH
CRUSADE IN EUROPE, Dwight Eisenhower, Heinemann, London, 1948
FLAMES IN THE FIELD – The Story of Four SOE Agents in Occupied
France, Rita Kramer, Michael Joseph, London, 1995.

Picture credits

The author acknowledges the generous contribution of illustra-
tions from: Brive, Cahors, Tulle and Limoges Resistance
Museums; Archives of Haute Vinne; Centre Jean Moulin; John
Fielding; Denis Chansigaud; Daphne Friele; Yale Kramer;
Maurice Lasvaux; Jacques Léonard; Dominique Lorimer; Guy
Pènaud; Jacques Poirier; Yves Soulignac; Special; Forces Club;
Taylor Picture Library; Alain d'Vomécourt; and Annieliese
Weidinger.

1ST SS PANZER REGIMENT SPECIAL HQ ORDER, DEPARTMENT OF THE LOT, 10.5.44.

SS OBERSTURMBANNFÜHRER MÜLLER,
CHIEF OF POLICE.

LARGE SCALE ACTION IN THE DEPARTMENT OF THE LOT

Beginning of the action: 10.5.44. around 6 pm, leaving from the staff HQ square.

Point of departure: CAUSSADE; staff of the 1st SS PANZER REGIMENT.
Arrive at the theatre of operations: 8 pm.

Taking part, among the members of the HQ group: as Chief of Police action:

SS Obersturmbannführer MÜLLER.
as adjutants:

SS Hauptscharführer:
>MARTEN
>JENSEN
>LIEBER

SS Oberscharführer:
>DECKER
>WONICKE
>RICHTER

SS Scharführer:
>DECKER
>NICKER
>ROBOLA
>THOMAS

SS Unterscharführer:
>MOHLEY
>JOHANNESSON
>RAUSCHER

SS Rottenführer:
MEINOL
WETTEMANN
GUNTHEE
SULZE
SCHAPFNER

SPECIAL ORDER FOR THE LARGE SCALE ACTION IN
THE DEPARTMENT OF THE LOT.

TARGET No. 1 is BLARS, at 30 kms north-east of
Cahors. In the vicinity of this place, is located a house
where the three chiefs of the organisation meet
everyday.
Apart from this, is located a big weapons dump
including about 1,500 sub-machine guns, 25 machine
guns, several hundreds of pounds of explosives, many
hand grenades, mortars, etc.

Committed unit: a Waffen SS Detachment.
Adjutant: SS Hauptscharführer: JENSEN.
Informer: ROY.
Dangerous moments in the Operation: about 2 kms
from the arms dump is located a Maquis of about 50
men. The approaches to the arms dump are mined.
Location of the mines is unknown. (See attached
copy). The informer ROY is able to lead the involved
unit unscathed across the minefield.

TARGET NO. 2. CABARETS-LAUZES, situated 14 kms
to the south west of Blars. In the forest of GRUAT-
SARL is located a Maquis of 150 Red Spaniards. The
Red Spanish Maquisards could remain in the caves.
These Spaniards have a tank-lorry of American origin
with 18,000 litres of petrol. This lorry is at about 2
kms from the camp, under the surveillance of a
sentry. In the event of an attack on the camp, this
sentry has the task of igniting a 2 meter fuse,
connected to a plastic bomb.

Committed unit: a Waffen SS Detachment.
Adjutant: SS Hauptscharführer: JENSEN.
Informer: ROY.
Information about the target which must be taken into account during the action.
The house where the terrorists meet everyday between 10 to 11 am and 8 to 10 pm is always under the surveillance of six terrorists who are equipped with machine guns in addition to sub-machine guns. The chief of the terrorists is called PHILIPPE, an ex-teacher at the grammar school of Cahors.

TARGET NO 3. SAINT-BRESSOU, about 32 kms north east from Blars. In the village, an isolated church could be the place of refuge of 50 to 60 Maquisards. Committed unit: a Waffen SS Detachment.
Adjutant: SS Unterscharführer: MOHLEY.
Informer: BOHN.

TARGET NO. 4. TERROU, 12 kms north from St-Bressou. An ammunition dump is located there. The munitions are hidden in several houses. Many terrorists are billeted in private houses. There are also large amounts of material such as equipment, shoes, soap, petrol, food, cigarettes, etc. In the circumstances, it could constitute the main Maquis camp. About 50 Maquisards could be found here. Committed unit: a Waffen SS Detachment.
Adjutant: SS Unterscharführer: LIEBER.

TARGET No 5. LATRONQUIERE, 25 kms north of Figeac. In this place are located about 50 terrorists, billeted uninhabited homes. The Maquisards possess 5 lorries, 3 motorcars, 3 motor cycles and 7 bicycles. Committed unit: a Waffen SS Detachment.
Adjutant: SS Oberscharführer: RICHTER
                              DECKER

TARGET NO 6. USSEL, 20 kms north of Cahors.
Between Ussel and Gigouzac, 3 kms from Ussel, and 5 kms from Gigouzac, two strong Maquis of about 30 to

40 men are located on the road. In one of these Maquis is a radio and telegraph operator in continuous liaison with England. The Maquisards are billeted in different houses situated on the right of the road. This group has the task of reinforcing other Maquis camps if they are attacked. They are particularly well armed and are in possession of light machine guns and mortars, in addition to STEN guns.
Committed unit: a Waffen SS Detachment.
Adjutant: SS Unterscharführer: JOHANNESSON.

TARGET NO 7. VAYRIERE, 30 kms north west from Cahors.
Near this locality is a farm where 4 wounded terrorists are being looked after. Beside that, there is a drop zone for enemy aircraft.
Committed unit: a Waffen SS Detachment.
Adjutant: SS Scharführer: NICKER.

TARGET NO 8. GRAMAT, 60 kms to the north east of Cahors. In this place are 60 terrorists. The Gendarmerie may have been disarmed. At the beginning of May, the terrorists are said to have demolished the post office, the telephone line and to have occupied the railway station.
In addition, the Maquis may have organised control over the hotels to get rid of suspected individuals, especially informers to the German intelligence forces. The French Gendarmerie is totally helpless. The population is in complete support of the guerilla bands.
Committed unit: a unit of the Waffen SS.
Adjutant: SS Scharführer: ROBOLA.
Informer: DEFRETELLE.

TARGET NO 9. SAINT-CÉRÉ, 35 kms to the north of Figeac. Near St-Céré is located a drop zone. In this area, some road blocks could have been organised by the terrorists. Outside of these, observation posts could have been established in the tops of trees. The road blocks could be within a radius of 50 kms.
Committed unit: Unit of Waffen SS.

Adjutant: SS Scharführer: THOMAS.
Informer: DEVIRUSEILLE.

TARGET NO 10. FIGEAC-CARDAILLAC, 10 kms north
of Figeac.
SOUSCEYRAC, ROCAMADOUR are riddled with
terrorists and Maquis camps.
The camps are located in a triangle situated to the
south east of ST-FELIX, north until SIRAM and to the
east in the direction of BRETENOUX on road number
140 as far as FIGEAC. This triangle is an area of
steep hills and chestnut tree woods.
Special attention must be paid to the airplane factory
RATIER at FIGEAC. In this factory, most of the young
workers are in the Maquis.
Committed unit: Unit of Waffen SS.
Adjutants: members of the Intelligence Services.

GENERAL SITUATION
People identified by our information services as being
suspected members of the Maquis, and in some cases,
chiefs, cannot be arrested during isolated actions.
It has been decided, with the chiefs of the Waffen SS,
to arrest ALL THE MEN OF THE DEPARTMENT OF
THE LOT and to bring them into a concentration
camp. The prisoners will be individually examined by
a special *Kommando* of the local Intelligence Service
which has to be created during this action and, to the
extent that these prisoners are found to be linked
with these events, they will be WORKED OVER by the
methods in force in the Security Service.
Other measures not indicated in this Special Order
and which may appear as necessary during the
actions, should be taken by the members of the
Intelligence Services on their own authority.

Situation: SS Obersturmbannführer MÜLLER

Appendix II

HOTELS AND RESTAURANTS

BAS SOLEIL B & B: La Réserve, 87400 St-Léonard-de-Noblat Tél: 05 55 56 18 39. You are with Mme Néline Jansen de Vomécort, on the site of the HQ of VENTRILOQUIST Circuit. (AA map ref. 124-C-2)

BELLAC Le Relais, Mortemart, Monts de Blond, on the D675. Tél: 05 55 68 12 09. Logis de France. (AA map ref. 110-C-6)

CAHORS L'Escargot, Boulevard Gambetta. Just near the Resistance Museum. Tél: 05 65 35 07 66. Try the Château Eugenié '95. (AA map ref. 152-C-4)

CHAMBERET Hotel de France, 5 Place du Marché. Tel: 05 55 98 30 14 (AA map ref. 125-E-4)

LA CROISILLE SUR BRIANCE Restaurant du Centre. Local cuisine. Tél: 05 55 71 78 33 (AA map ref. 124-D-4)

GOURDON Hôtellerie de la Bouriane, Place du Foirail. 100 years of history. Logis de France. Tél: 05 65 41 16 37 (AA map ref. 152-C-2)

GROLÉJAC Hôtel du Pont. Site of the battle, Proprietor: M Jardel. Tél: 50 53 28 15 94. (AA map ref. 136-B-6)

LIMOGES Le Moulin de la Gorce, La Roche-l'Abeille. On the D704, south of Limoges. Relais & Châteaux. 1st class. Tél: 05 55 00 70 66. (AA map ref. 124-B-5)

MARTEL Le Turenne/Le Quercy. Logis de France. NESTOR's 'safe house'. Tél: 05 65 37 30 30 (AA map ref. 138-D-5)

MONTAUBAN Le Lion d'Or, Avenue de Mayenne, near the Station. Ambience of the period, good local cuisine. Tél: 05 63 20 04 04. (AA map ref. 167-E-2)

ORADOUR La Glane, Place Gen de Gaulle. Tél: 05 55 03 10 43. (AA map ref. 123-H-2)

TERRASSON Le Vieux Moulin, Avenue Charles de Gaulle. Tél: 05 53 50 26 75. (AA map ref. 138-B-3)

A little to your west, in the direction of the Bordeaux wine country, try Jacques de la Bardonnie's excellent biological wine at his Château St-Antoine-de-Breuilh. (136-B-6) When we visited there the original wireless cables for transmissions to London still dangled from an upstairs window.

INDEX